MOMENTS
OF TRUTH

MOMENTS OF TRUTH

Tony Wainwright
and Mike Celizic

NEW AMERICAN LIBRARY

NEW AMERICAN LIBRARY
Published by New American Library, a division of
Penguin Putnam Inc., 375 Hudson Street,
New York, New York 10014, U.S.A.
Penguin Books Ltd, 27 Wrights Lane,
London W8 5TZ, England
Penguin Books Australia Ltd, Ringwood,
Victoria, Australia
Penguin Books Canada Ltd, 10 Alcorn Avenue,
Toronto, Ontario, Canada M4V 3B2
Penguin Books (N.Z.) Ltd, 182–190 Wairau Road,
Auckland 10, New Zealand

Penguin Book Ltd, Registered Offices:
Harmondsworth, Middlesex, England

Published by New American Library, a division of Penguin Putnam Inc.

First Printing, April 2001
10   9   8   7   6   5   4   3   2   1

 REGISTERED TRADEMARK—MARCA REGISTRADA

LIBRARY OF CONGRESS CATALOGING-IN-PUBLICATION DATA:
Wainwright, Tony.
Moments of truth / Tony Wainwright and Mike Celizic.
p.   cm.
ISBN 0-451-40928-0 (alk. paper)
1. Life change events.   2. Conduct of life.   I. Celizic, Mike.   II. Title.

BJ1597.W34 2001
920'.009'045—dc21
00-066209

Printed in the United States of America
Set in Galliard
Designed by Leonard Telesca

Printed in the United States of America

ACKNOWLEDGMENTS

I want to express my sincere appreciation and admiration for the wonderful work done by my coauthor, Mike Celizic. He did the hard part, and did it beautifully. Thanks, Mike.

I cannot thank Barry Farber, my good friend and primary agent, enough. It was his dedication that made this book happen. So, too, many thanks to Rob Robertson, my other agent, whose wisdom and editorial skills were invaluable. Also thanks to Ellen Edwards, my editor at New American Library, and Liz Perl, publicity director at NAL. She not only headed our PR efforts, but was a champion for the project from the beginning.

My thanks to the dozens of people who graciously gave their time to be interviewed and then gave even more of their time to review their stories.

My special thanks to Marybeth, my wife, who put up with all the calls and trips.

Also, I want to thank Nadine Brodie-Allen, my assistant, who lived this one with great grace.

Finally, my thanks to God, Who has given me the conviction and the strength to continue on—no matter what.

—*Tony Wainwright*

Contents

PART TWO
Daily Struggles Often Bring Moments of Truth 65

PART THREE
Moments of Truth Lie in Discovering Who You Really Are 119

PART FOUR
Small Steps Can Bring You to a Moment of Truth 157

PART FIVE
Moments of Truth Lie in Realizing
What Really Matters 185

AFTERWORD
The Next Moment of Truth:
A Final Word from Tony 223

INTRODUCTION

Back in the 1960s, I began the "Moment of Truth" journey. Over the next twenty-five years, I attempted to correspond with well-known, interesting people, asking them to share their experiences with me and, ultimately, my readers.

When I began, I had limited resources and no leverage. I was simply a young man with an idea. So my letters were direct. I had had a life-changing experience. Perhaps other people had had one as well.

In all, I wrote to some three hundred people—all over the world.

To my delight, I received replies from many of them. Some responses were rich, rewarding, and remarkable, including those from Thomas Merton (the contemplative priest), Prime Minister Sean LeMass (of Ireland), and Henry

Moore (the world-famous sculptor). Some were unexpected: I was thoroughly investigated by the FBI before receiving a letter from Director J. Edgar Hoover.

Some letters were surprising: Somerset Maugham wrote that he was old and tired and wanted to be left alone to die. Eleanor Roosevelt said she hadn't had a "Moment of Truth" in her life.

By 1989 the book was finally ready to be published. A small house brought it out, and with the advertising and promotion that I contributed to the project, many people bought and enjoyed the book.

My proceeds went to charity.

Two years ago, a good friend of mine, Barry Farber, suggested that a new and expanded version might do well. This time there would be interviews (no letters) and the people would be more of a "mix," more regular people facing problems in their lives.

Barry is an author, motivational speaker, and TV personality. He is a "doer." In no time, Barry had lined up Rob Robertson, a top literary agent, and had meetings set up at several of the best New York City publishing houses. Rob had suggested we bring in Mike Celizic, a freelance writer, to work with me. Within a couple of months we signed a contract with New American Library , a division of Penguin Putnam Inc.

And so we began.

I made up a list of people I wanted to interview and a corresponding list of people I knew who might help by way of introduction. Soon I was off and running. My doctor,

Sid Neimark, introduced me to Celine Dion. She gave us a wonderful, warm interview. A lovely, caring lady.

Chris Evans, an old friend of mine from Dallas, told his story. It is an especially heartening one since I know what he's gone through to get where he is today.

So, too, with Father Paul Sheridan. How many children he's saved through Boys Hope Girls Hope! His was the most clearly perceived calling, a Moment of Truth that has positively affected many, many lives.

What I have learned is that most of us have experienced one or more "defining moments." Some are dramatic, others less so. Even the people who claim that they have never experienced a Moment of Truth can often look back at their lives and identify important turning points.

Some of the people I approached were not willing to share their life stories. One man I interviewed refused to discuss the many personal and business crises I knew he had experienced. I respected his wishes. I conducted the interview but didn't include his story in the book.

It's not easy to "go public" with what are often very private, personal struggles. Yet I believe that when we do share our stories we realize how much they have in common. And in sharing, we gain strength from one another. To those who did open their hearts to me, I say a sincere thank-you.

Suffering is universal. But I believe that in most instances, people can overcome their suffering and go on with their lives. Often, they are better, stronger, more caring people for the experience.

So my hope is that *Moments of Truth* will be a positive force for each of you. As you read these stories of how others faced life-defining situations, perhaps you'll find renewed strength and encouragement to face your own challenges.

—*Tony Wainwright*

TONY'S MOMENT OF TRUTH

It was a big old brick and stone building on the South Side of Chicago, in what in the 1960s we used to call a "marginal neighborhood." The sign over the door read MISERECORDIA—Latin for merciful heart—and it was staffed by nursing nuns.

This is where I came every day for the better part of a year, because this is where they sent my baby to die. It is where, face-to-face with death and loss and the harsh reality of life, I faced my Moment of Truth, a moment that has defined and driven my life ever since. And with it came the realization that I was not alone.

My daughter's name was Mary, and she never came home, never met her three-year-old sister, never suckled at her mother's breast, never filled a home with gurgles and coos and the wonderful smell of a baby fresh from the bath.

These were the things I thought of when I came to Miserecordia and walked into the big room where the dying babies lived out their brief and heartbreaking lives under the
care of the nursing nuns.

The room was high-ceilinged in the manner of old insti-
tutions, and it was big enough to hold twenty-five or
thirty-five cribs with aisles between them and tables for the
machines and medicines used in the care of the babies. And
in every crib lay somebody's precious baby, come there
only incidentally to eat and cry and defecate and sleep, and
primarily to die out of sight and mind of polite society, that
life leaving not so much as a ripple in anyone's routine except those of their agonized parents and the wonderful
nuns who cared for them.

What I remember nearly forty years later is the other-
worldly ambience of the place. Mostly, I remember white.
Not just the floor and walls and ceiling, but everything was
white—the cribs, the sheets, the habits of the nuns themselves, the nuns who worked with such patience and cheer
and love. From the ceiling hung old-fashioned fans that ro-
tated lazily, churning the humid air, mixing it with the
smell of medicine and babies and the enormous sadness
that permeated the room. Looking back, I see it as something out of a Stanley Kubrick movie, a place not of this
earth.

And, truly, it wasn't of this earth, wasn't natural in any
way. It was a perversion of nature. Heaven's waiting room.

My beautiful baby Mary was born with spina bifida, an
opening at the base of the spine for which there was at that
time no treatment that could prolong life beyond a year or

so. I had no idea what it was in 1962, had never heard of such a thing. But I had not heard of a lot of things back then when I was young. The world was my oyster, and tragedy and hard luck were things that happened in the movies or to other people, but not to me.

Chicago was as much of a hometown as I had experienced growing up. I was an only child, the son of a radio scriptwriter. It was quite a way to grow up, gypsylike and exciting, first living in California, then following my father's muse to Chicago, where he scripted shows of every description—comedy, drama, soap operas, serials.

The income was never certain, coming in spurts from shows that were contracted for in thirteen-week chunks, with my father never knowing if the next three months would bring renewal or a nervous scramble for another assignment. It was a feast-or-famine existence, one that didn't allow for home owning or even a long-term lease in an apartment.

I spent the best years of my youth in residential hotel suites in Chicago, rented by the month. For a kid, it was fun. I had my own room, and from time to time I shared it with guests and friends of my parents. I remember one time my parents asking me if I would share with a radio actor who had gone a gin or two over the line. In the morning I met Red Skelton, who I thought was just a funny guy who slept it off in the next bed.

As I got older, I decided I wanted to be a syndicated newspaper columnist, which was as glamorous a media job as there was in the early 1950s, and I went to the University of Colorado to study journalism. But they weren't handing out syndicated columns to kids fresh out of school, and not wanting to settle for less, I found myself with a job in advertising. It was writing, and it was creative, and it suited me. I was good at it, too, and while I wasn't exactly a human dynamo, I liked the work.

It went that way into my late twenties—a pretty good life for a young man in postwar America. And it got better when I went out to Los Angeles with a gang of other young adults at the invitation of a mutual friend who was in show business out there. He took us all over to Jack Webb's house for a party, and it was there that I met a stunningly pretty girl who was also from Chicago. Her name was Anne. I met her on Tuesday and proposed on Friday. She said yes.

So we went back to Chicago—she the daughter of a prominent and wealthy business family and me the son of a gypsy writer—and got on with the business of living our version of the American Dream. I worked my way up the advertising ladder, and Anne, who got pregnant on our honeymoon, waited for the baby and kept house in our little apartment.

I wasn't making a lot of money, and since I'd grown up in furnished rooms, that's where we began our married life. It was a tiny apartment at the wrong end of Rush Street in a building that we shared with colorful and worldly people. Looking back, I realize that some of the ladies worked the streets and the men worked the bars and the back rooms and the racetracks. But they were great to us, and it all seemed awfully exciting.

The principal attraction of the apartment itself was that it was cheap and it was furnished. The furniture was that old dark mahogany stuff, probably from the twenties or thirties, and it fit right in because the apartment itself was hemmed in by taller buildings so that it got less light than the inside of a cow's stomach. But when our first baby, Colleen, arrived, she lit up the place better than a set of klieg lights.

Life was good. Our neighbors were unaccustomed to real family life, and so they fussed and cooed over Colleen as if she were the only baby on earth.

Then I went to Mexico for vacation, and nothing was ever the same again.

It started as a case of dysentery, which is what you were supposed to get when you went to foreign countries. Since I had never been sick in my life, I figured it would go away on its own or, at worst, after a couple of shots of Kaopectate. But it didn't go away. Finally I went to a doctor and started a series of tests and treatments that went on for quite a while before they realized it wasn't dysentery. I had Crohn's disease, which attacks the digestive tract. There's no living with the disease. It ties your insides in agonizing knots and sucks the life out of you.

No one knew how you got it or how to cure it. If it didn't clear up on its own, the alternative was to open me up, take out the diseased sections of my bowel, sew it back together, and wait for it to heal. Oh, yes, and while it was healing I would have to use an ostomy, in which they route your bowels to an opening in your side and an attached bag.

It didn't clear up on its own.

Call it Strike One.

I went ahead with the surgery and the long hospital stay that went with it. By the time I was released, I was down to 130 pounds from my normal weight of 170. None of my clothes fit, and when I buttoned my shirt collars, my neck stuck through like a pencil in a wedding ring. I didn't have money for new clothes, so I snugged my ties up as tightly as I could, and looking like the walking dead, I went back to work.

But in the two months that I had been on my back, the ad company I was working for discovered it didn't need me anymore. I wasn't exactly fired, but there wasn't a job waiting for me.

Call it Strike Two.

The months that followed were awful. Every day I pulled my best clothes over what was left of my body and hit the streets looking for work. There were plenty of ad firms in Chicago, but none were hiring. The closest I got to a job for a long time was a horrible little place that looked at my credentials and told me I was of a higher caliber than their usual applicant. They said they'd put me on the draw. When I asked what that was, they said they'd advance me some money, and when I landed an account, I'd have to pay them back.

That's crazy, I told them. It's not professional. I need a salary.

The closing door practically hit me on the way out.

I wouldn't apply for unemployment—and never did. I had too much pride for that. But I did allow my parents to put me on what amounted to an allowance. It wasn't much, but we paid the rent and bought groceries. I promised I'd pay the loan back, and I did.

We had a little Volkswagen Beetle, and on weekends we'd visit Anne's folks at their mansion in the country. It was an utterly different world from anything I had ever experienced, a world of society events and debutante balls, and I never felt part of it. My in-laws were wonderful to me and solicitous of my well-being, but I hated their asking me every week if I'd had any luck finding a job. Every time that I had to say I hadn't, it hurt worse.

During that time, Anne got pregnant again, a development that we both greeted with joy. Colleen was about two years old and as cute as a child can get. The prospect of another baby gave me something miraculous and wonderful to look forward to, and as the new life inside Anne grew, so did my own spirit.

I finally got another job. The light was finally getting brighter at the end of my personal tunnel. When the time came near for the baby, we got ready to send Colleen to my parents, who still lived downtown, while Anne and I went to the hospital. So when Anne woke me in the dead of a hot summer night and told me it was time, we were ready.

We dropped Colleen off and took a cab to the hospital, just half a dozen or so blocks away. In those days, there was no such thing as Lamaze classes, and if anyone had suggested that fathers should be in the labor and delivery rooms, they would have been locked up. So when they took Anne off for the mystery of birth, they sent me to the waiting room, where I joined a small group of prospective fathers. With nothing to do but wait and worry, we did exactly what the stereotype of the time portrayed—chain-smoked cigarettes and paced.

However long the wait was, it seemed like aeons. Finally, Anne's obstetrician came to the door and said he wanted to talk to me.

I thought nothing of it because this was how it worked. The doctor came and took you out and told you that the baby was born, it was a boy or girl, and mother and baby were doing fine. I was so high on the emotion of the moment and so into my own thoughts, it didn't register that the doctor was subdued and serious.

He walked me away from everyone and down a hospital corridor, and there, with the flat glare of fluorescent lights and the smell of disinfectant pounding home the reality of where I was, he put his hand on my shoulder and said, "Tony, there's a problem with the baby."

A problem? My heart was racing. *What kind of problem? Is Anne okay? Is the baby alive?* A thousand thoughts raced through my mind. Through a haze, I heard the words "spina bifida."

What's that? Is it bad?

Yes, it was bad.

How bad? How do you treat it?

I didn't understand. There was no treatment. She was born with an exposed spinal cord at the base of her spine. The child was paralyzed from the waist down. The condition would cause fluid to build up in the brain—hydrocephalism. My baby would probably not see her first birthday.

I was in emotional shock, all numb inside, the outside world a fog, the words hitting me like hammers but not registering except as dull and distant thuds. I asked if I could see Anne and the baby, and the doctor said I could.

Walking into the room was terrifying. I didn't know what I would see, didn't know if my baby would look like some sort of monster, had no idea how I would react, how Anne would be.

What I saw was probably the worst thing imaginable. Anne, worn-out and drugged and still beautiful, was propped up holding the prettiest baby I had ever seen. She was a perfect little Irish angel, with a little round head, beautiful blue eyes, and a little button nose. Surely a child so pretty could not be doomed. Anyone could see that she was perfect just by looking at her. She was wrapped up in blankets. The damaged spine didn't show. Her lifeless legs were hidden.

That was when I finally lost it, and Anne with me. We held on to each other and cried out our grief and pain until we had used up all our tears and someone gently led me away and took the baby back to the nursery.

But the agony wasn't over. From the hospital, I called Anne's folks and my folks and her siblings and everyone who had to be called. My mother wailed. Her mother wailed. Inside, the gnawing question that is never answered—*Why me? Why us?*—pounded at my emotions, and behind it, the other self-accusing question, *Is God punishing me?*

The doctors were wonderful to me. Anne's obstetrician contacted our family doctor, who came over and talked to me, explaining what had happened and what would happen and that it wasn't my fault or Anne's. He told me as gently as he could that when Anne came home, Mary would not come with her; Mary would never come home. I absorbed what I could and finally, thanking him for all his help and time and caring, I left.

I have no recollection of how I got home or how long it took or what time it was when I arrived. Colleen was with her grandparents, and without her or Anne, the little apartment was a dark and depressing place, offering no comfort. I suppose it's fortunate that I've never been a drinker, or I might have crawled in a bottle right then and never crawled out again.

Call it Strike Three.

As I said, until then I hadn't been a particularly energetic employee. I did well enough, but I wasn't a real go-getter. I wasn't driven. But the combination of everything that had happened to me made me stop and take inventory of where I was, what I wanted to be, and how I would get there. It was probably as much a defense mechanism and a form of self-therapy as anything else, but I decided that I would make up for all the time I felt I had wasted and throw myself into my job with everything I had.

After what I'd been through, I knew with certainty that nothing is given to you, and life does not come with guarantees. I couldn't control the disease and what happened to my baby, but I could control how hard I worked and what I accomplished. Maybe I wasn't the brightest guy in the advertising business, but I was determined that I would be the hardest-working.

I started going to work at four in the morning to get a head start on everyone else. In those days, the business world ran on a nine-to-five schedule, and the three-martini lunch was in style. I went on a predawn to postdusk schedule, burying myself, my grief, and everything else under work.

When work was done, I went to see Mary at Miserecordia, saying hello to the nuns, who glided among the cribs, seemingly borne a few inches above the ground by their enormous winged headdresses. Whether for a couple of minutes or an hour, I went almost every day to sit by Mary, to look at her face, stroke her cheek, talk to her.

As it was with the other babies, the fluid was slowly filling her brain cavity. Every day her little head was a tiny bit larger from the pressure of the fluid. The whole room was filled with babies like that, in different stages of the disease, their heads slowly getting bigger and more grotesque until finally the pressure crushed the brain and brain stem, and the baby died. So I would come in one day and there would be Baby A, Baby B, and Baby C, and I would come in the next day and Baby B would be gone. Then Baby A. Then Baby C. And in their places other brand-new babies, as cute and perfect-looking as my Mary had been, just embarked on their brief voyages through life.

That was my life—work, Mary, home, with barely time to see Colleen and Anne, always with my load of sorrow. Ironically, as this was going on, I was working on various ad campaigns, selling things with sweetness and light and good cheer. The biggest campaign I worked on at the time was for Illinois Bell Telephone, and it was called "Make Someone Happy." It was a huge success and Ma Bell took the campaign national. And every day I went to watch Mary die.

About ten months after she had been born, the nuns called and said that Mary had passed peacefully away. Her suffering was over.

Eventually, my pain would dull as well. Anne got pregnant again, and we had another healthy, wonderful daughter. But I never forgot the lesson I had learned and the decision I had made when everything was closing in on me. From the day I decided to outwork everyone else, I have never stopped.

At some point during Mary's brief life, I realized that what I had faced was my Moment of Truth—a clear and undeniable point in time when I confronted a crisis and was forced to make decisions that defined the rest of my life. As I thought about it, I figured that others must experience similar moments, and that realization began another life-long quest—to find those people and write about their own Moments of Truth. This book is the result of that quest.

PART ONE

Looking Beyond Yourself Can Lead to a Moment of Truth

The rewards we get from life are directly related to what we give to others.

This is not a belief. It is the truth.

John Donne, the metaphysical poet, wrote: "No man is an island, entire to himself."

We live in an era in which the individual is celebrated. If it feels good, do it. Look out for Number One. These are the slogans of our time.

When you think only of yourself, that is all you have. But when you expand your world to embrace others, when you see that we are all one, you begin to sow seeds that will blossom and grow and reward you a thousandfold.

When I went through a series of personal challenges capped by the death of my infant daughter nearly forty years ago, my life changed dramatically. I resolved that from her death would come good. I wasn't sure how that would happen, but I knew that I would make it so.

The tragedy changed me in many ways. I became highly sensitive to people with physical problems. When I saw people with such afflictions, I extended myself time and time again. Out of that grew my involvement in helping to fund a transplant center at Baylor University Medical Center in Texas and to see to it that people who did not have the medical insurance or the money to afford transplants could get them.

Several years ago, when the hospital held a dinner for those who had received lifesaving transplants, I looked around the room at the forty or so people who were celebrating new leases on life, and it flashed through my mind that had I not gone through what I had, those people would not be at those tables.

Call it whatever you want—altruism, giving back, charity, empathy. I call it the hand of God that led me to that place through my own suffering.

I had a choice to make. I could go on living as I had been, putting my daughter's suffering and death out of my mind, or I could honor her memory and look beyond my own suffering by trying to help others. It was my Moment of Truth. I believe that God led me to that defining moment. But I had a choice, just the same.

I am reminded of a story I heard of two brothers, close in age, the product of the same childhood made horrible by an abusive, alcoholic father. One of the brothers became a tremendous success and spent his life helping children whose parents were alcoholics. When asked why he chose that path, he replied, "What would you expect from someone who had a father like mine?" The second brother became a drunk himself, turned to crime, and ended up in prison, a hardened, incorrigible criminal. Asked why he did what he did, he answered, "What would you expect from someone who had a father like mine?"

Each had a choice and each took a path—one selfless, one selfish. The following stories are about six others who made such a decision. In each case—John McCain, Father Paul Sheridan, Anne Meagher Northup, Mitchell S. Rosenthal, and Henry and Patricia King—the person or persons involved were drawn toward a higher calling. Each faced a Moment of Truth and felt what I call the hand of God pointing toward the path of greater resistance. By taking that road, they have made the world a better place for all of us.

SENATOR JOHN MCCAIN

No one survives what John McCain went through without a strong motivating power. At some point, the mere will to live is not enough. There must be something to live for. For John, that was his country and everything for which it stands. The rule of law, democracy, human rights, and freedom. It is what all politicians say they believe in, but few prove their belief in quite the way John did.

John McCain's Moment of Truth was five years in the making. He believed that his suffering was not just for him, but for the country he served and loved. What he endured is a testament to selflessness and sacrifice for the greater good.

The story is familiar to most Americans. John McCain spent more than five years in a North Vietnamese prisoner-of-war camp in which every day brought pain, sensory deprivation, brainwashing, and despair. During every minute of his ordeal, John knew that he could leave anytime he wanted. He could call his guards and say, "I want to go home" and within 48 hours he would be on a plane back to the United States. Yet he refused the offer of freedom.

John was shot down on October 27, 1967. He was hospitalized and in the summer of 1968 transferred to Colonel Bai's Hao Lo prison camp—nicknamed the Hanoi Hilton.

A year earlier, the North Vietnamese had begun releasing American POWs in groups of three from time to time. Ho Chi Minh had discovered the power of public relations. At the time, most Americans were still firmly behind the war, but the nation's mood was changing rapidly. There had always been a protocol to releasing prisoners—the gravely ill or injured were released first, followed by those who had been in captivity the longest.

But Bai told John he didn't have to wait his turn. He could leave immediately. Go home. Reunite with his wife and family. Leave the horrid war and god-awful jungle behind forever.

John knew the alternative without being told—refuse the offer, and his life would be filled with physical and psychological torture.

John turned the offer down.

"My Moment of Truth," he tells me years later.

Look around the United States Senate, where John represents the State of Arizona, and try to imagine another politician who wouldn't take the offer in a heartbeat. Heck, look in the White House and ask the same question. Look inside yourself. What would you do? Freedom or unspeak-able torture?

For most people, John's decision was a no-brainer. The deal—Take it, please!—is freedom.

Colonel Bai thought he knew what John would decide. The man who ran North Vietnam's prisoner-of-war camps had been told that John was a spoiled flyboy who would accept freedom without looking back. Bai thought that the word "sacrifice" wasn't a part of the American's vocabulary.

By coincidence, John's father, a career naval officer, had been appointed commander of the Pacific Fleet soon after John was captured. When he learned of his father's promotion, John understood why Colonel Bai was pretending to be nice to him. If John took early release, ahead of other Americans who were more badly injured or who had been in captivity longer, North Vietnam's propaganda machine could put out the word that, in America, privilege and social standing count, that American democracy is a lie. And Bai would be sure that every American prisoner and every enlisted man slogging through rice paddies knew that the admiral's kid had gotten preferential treatment. It would be a double blow against America, a cut to the nation's professed ideals and a belly punch to the morale of its fighting men.

Imagine the headlines. DOWNED FLYER USES DADDY'S IN-FLUENCE TO ESCAPE. U.S. MILITARY PUTS KINSHIP AHEAD OF DUTY. The effect on the ordinary grunts in the trenches in that awful war would be devastating. What kind of country are they fighting for when an admiral's son gets special treatment and a pipe fitter's son has to rot in a jungle hell?

When John had signed on with the Navy, he had sworn to uphold the military's Code of Conduct. Composed after the Korean War, during which the Chinese had succeeded in breaking the will of many American prisoners, the Code of Conduct did not require prisoners to resist torture forever, but it did impose standards of conduct for prisoners of war.

"I will not accept preferential release," John says today, quoting from the Code. "I will only accept release by order of capture. The sick and the injured must be released first. I will wait my turn." He told Colonel Bai that, and Bai told him to think about it. In the meantime, Bai made sure that a letter from one of John's friends—a major in the military— got through to him. The letter begged him to reconsider and to accept early release.

When the colonel called John before him again, Bai handed John a letter from his wife. In it, she wrote how she hoped and prayed that he could come home. Bai repeated his offer.

John refused again. Though he didn't know it, his second refusal marked the last letter he would see from his wife for more than five years.

Finally, in December 1970, Colonel Bai made one more attempt to get John to accept release. It had been two and a half years since his capture, and John understood well the harsh reality of life in the prison camp. And he knew how much worse it could be if he did not cooperate.

Yet John refused. Enraged, Bai kicked over a chair in his office and stared into the burning eyes of the emaciated prisoner.

John saw in the man's gaze a grudging admiration for

the captive's resolve. "I understand better than you imagine," Bai said before sending McCain away. It was the last time the men saw each other.

At last, Bai realized that there was more to this pilot than he had imagined. He had underestimated the will of this "spoiled" American.

That was when the serious torture began. Guards came to John's cell and beat him unconscious, revived him, then beat him again. They conducted endless interrogation sessions, deprived John of sleep, kept him in isolation.

John doesn't often talk about those years, and at the mention of his experiences in the Hanoi Hilton, a cloud passes over his face and it's clear that the nightmares will never leave him.

It took an enormous effort to rebuild his life when he finally came home after the war, to face his terrors and to enter politics. At the same time, I understand why he often doesn't hesitate to buck the leadership of his Republican Party. He has faced far more dangerous opponents.

But the John McCain who grew up to challenge fellow Republicans over such issues as campaign finance reform and Big Tobacco is not the John McCain who entered the Navy as a young man and went off to Vietnam to fight in a war that changed the nation no less dramatically than it changed him.

John's pedigree as a naval officer was impeccable. His grandfather, John S. McCain Sr., and his father, John S. McCain Jr., were admirals, and John followed in their footsteps, entering the U.S. Naval Academy in 1954.

But as Jake Tapper wrote in *Salon* magazine in 1999,

"McCain has been brash ever since he was a kid. From high school through the Naval Academy, McCain was in an extended rebel-without-a-clue phase, always more interested in the three B's—booze, brawls, and broads."

John finished fifth from the bottom of his class at the academy, not a particularly propitious start. But combat pilots have never been the most placid members of society. In any event, if John had the stuff that heroes are made of, it didn't show in his early life. No one knows how a person will react when faced with a choice between life and honor until that moment arrives. The fact that there are so few genuine heroes shows how rare the conditions are that create them. The vast majority of people never face the kind of decision that John did. Such an ordeal is seldom sought out. It is thrust upon us. One might think that John's decision was gut-wrenching, particularly for one who broke all the rules when not in the cockpit doing the job his country asked him to do. But for John the choice was easy.

"I wouldn't consider any kind of release," he says. "They'd have to drag me out of there."

By the time his captors finished with him, John didn't have a scrap of macho flyer self-image left. After endless beatings, he finally signed a "confession" to war crimes.

He wasn't the first and wouldn't be the last to do that, and the military, which has come to understand the effects of such brutal and continued torture, doesn't consider such a "confession" to be a violation of the Code of Conduct. John resisted with every fiber of his being, and when there was nothing left, he did what any of us would have done. He signed the paper.

John would like to say his experience turned him into a perfect individual, motivated only by the most noble of principles and ambitions. "But that's not true," he said. "I was privileged to serve in the company of heroes. I failed in prison . . . and as I continue to strive to do the right thing . . . I fail very frequently."

From the lips of a politician, such humility is rare.

John understands how his decision and the years of torture made him what he is today. Having experienced the total destruction of his pride, he can make his way through the corridors of power without fear. And he can stand up for his beliefs, knowing that they have been tested in the harshest arena. That is what his Moment of Truth has given him.

FATHER PAUL SHERIDAN, S.J.

To choose the life of a Catholic priest is to choose a life of obedience. But obedience to whom? Father Paul Sheridan always intended to obey his religious superiors who represented the Church. Obedience seemed an easy assignment, for the Church had chosen for him a welcome path of intellectual achievement and a life involved in teaching and foreign affairs. It would have been a good life, a life envied even by those who were not religious, a life that might have introduced him to world leaders. But he found that God had other plans for him. To obey his superiors would lead to a life of prestige and comfort. To obey God would lead to a life of sacrifice, but, ultimately, to enormous rewards. His Moment of Truth came when he listened to a higher calling.

Father Paul Sheridan, S.J., didn't set out to change the world, one life at a time, but he was given a choice during his senior year of college that turned out to be his Moment of Truth. Today, because he followed his inner voice, more than two hundred children in the United States, Latin America, and Ireland are rescued each year and given the chance of a brighter future.

The organization that Father Paul founded in St. Louis in 1974 is Boys Hope Girls Hope, and every year it takes kids who are homeless, abused, neglected, starving, despairing, angry—the entire litany of horrors visited upon children—and gives them a safe home, the loving support of houseparents, the best schooling available, nourishing meals, and medical and dental care. Most of all, Boys Hope Girls Hope gives them a reason to live.

Father Paul Sheridan has taken kids who were broken and defeated, kids who had given up on everything, and helped them to become doctors, lawyers, engineers, accountants, business leaders, teachers, artists, police officers, and officers in the armed forces.

As remarkable and inspiring as Boys Hope Girls Hope is, the story of how it came into being, of how a young Jesuit Scholastic found his calling, is even more so. It is a wonderful story about a wonderful man.

Like so many Catholic boys educated in parochial schools, Paul, who was born in 1943, entertained thoughts of becoming a priest when he grew up. But he admits, "I wasn't a saint. I was very sports-oriented. My dad made sure I read books, but I preferred sports."

It was in high school, when he fell under the direction of the Jesuits, that his vocation returned, stronger than ever. On graduation, he enrolled at the University of St.

Louis, a Jesuit school, with the intention of becoming a priest.

He was a scholastic, and still a long way from being ordained, but his course was set. As he entered his senior year, his superiors decided to send him to graduate school at Georgetown University in Washington, D.C., to study for a doctorate in public service in preparation for a career as a teacher. It was a terrific assignment, and Paul eagerly looked forward to it.

But Paul had always enjoyed working with kids and during his senior year at St. Louis, he became involved with a program called Full Achievement, in the worst inner-city neighborhood in St. Louis. "We had girls and boys from the ages of seven to eighteen," he says. "We had Brownies, Girl Scouts, Boy Scouts, Eagle Scouts—maybe 220 kids. We took over two abandoned schools at night and tutored the kids and taught them sports. In the summers, we made sure they got to ball games. Twice a month on Saturdays, the tutors were supposed to take the kids to some event or activity."

Each tutor was assigned to work one night a week during the school year. Paul coached the kids' basketball team. After each two-hour session, the tutors walked the children home before going back to campus.

Paul graduated at the end of May 1969, and he went one last night to work at Full Achievement. It was either Tuesday or Wednesday, as he remembers, and he was due to leave for Georgetown on Saturday. He was eager to go, ready to get on with his life.

He walked his kids home and arrived at his last stop, a

ramshackle frame house where two of the youngsters lived. "When you walked in, you could smell the urine," he says. "It was crowded, and there was no heat or air-conditioning. In the winter, the kids would lie on the kitchen floor in front of the oven. That was their source of heat. The mother was doing the best she could, but they were very, very poor and she had problems of her own."

Paul said good-bye to the kids and told them he was going away and wouldn't be back. He walked out of the house toward a car driven by another student who would take them the eight miles back to the university.

"That's when it happened." His voice fills with wonder as he speaks to me thirty years later. "I think it was an act of God. He said to me, 'You can't leave these kids here.' "

"It was a stunning and very exciting revelation," he says. "I remember feeling that this couldn't be—that in one moment my whole course in life could be decided. I had no rancor. I wasn't upset knowing that I would not be going to Georgetown after all. It was just a puzzlement, a 'Wow! It happened.'

"Instead of walking back to the car, I just walked back to the university. I walked eight miles just to think it over, to understand what the heck was happening," he goes on. "My heart was pounding. There was absolute certainty that God wanted me to work with these kids. I didn't know how, but in my heart, I knew it would happen.

"It was an instantaneous invitation by God to take care of these kids," he continues. "It was so powerful and so uplifting. Here I can't wait to get to Georgetown, and in a moment, I can't leave these kids. But that wasn't bad. It was a joyous thing. My mind kept asking how it could be, but my heart was saying, 'Yes. It's the right thing to do.'

"It was uplifting, exhilarating. But at the same time elusive in the sense of how I would put all this together. I knew deep down I'd get permission, but how would I do it?"

One senses that mere words cannot describe everything that Paul felt that night. Certainly, many people in his place might have fought off the voice he heard and gone on with their lives. When the future is so clear and so attractive, it is hard to hear a Moment of Truth. After all, we are most comfortable when we know where we are going, how we will get there, and how we will pay our way. As romantic as the idea of adventure sounds, when faced with the real thing, we tend to choose certainty.

Listening to Father Paul's story makes me think of pioneers and explorers striking off into the unknown. That is precisely what Father Paul did, and his journey shows that one does not have to discover new lands to be a pioneer, that all great journeys are journeys of the spirit and begin not with a single step but with an idea and the courage to bring the idea to life.

We all have dreams. What separates this brave man from most of us is that he found the courage to act.

In one moment, his life lay before him, straight and sure. In the next, that path was replaced by what ancient cartographers called "terra incognita" and marked with dragons and whirlpools.

Do we really want to go there? With the clarity of faith, Father Paul recognized that the voice speaking to him posed not only a challenge but also an opportunity. He opened himself to a higher authority and accepted the task put in front of him.

Father Paul says that when he is praying, "There are moments when you feel God is sitting right next to you. But the inner peace and joy and excitement of that night has never been replicated."

He felt no sense of loss because he would not be going to Georgetown, only joy in his calling. He turned it over in his mind during that long walk through the St. Louis night back to campus. When he finally returned home, he woke his superior up to tell him what had happened.

"You won't believe this," he began, and then told his story.

The priest listened, and when Paul was done, he said, "You know you have to act on this."

"I know," Paul replied.

The only hitch was getting the approval of the order's superiors in New York, but Paul knew in his heart that they would not stand in his way, and they didn't. Okay, they said. Stay in St. Louis. Take two years to get your master's. Continue to work with Full Achievement. And draw up a plan for what you want to do.

His assignment now was to give his idea form and substance. Like any explorer, he could not simply launch himself into the future. To do that would be to risk failure. He had to plan for the journey, choose an initial destination, decide how to get there, determine what he would need along the way.

The Moment of Truth became a process. Paul didn't

know exactly where it would take him. He had to figure that out on his own. He was able to do it because he knew the mission he had been given was good and noble and right, because he believed.

Instead of living at the university, Paul moved into the inner city during those two years and continued to develop programs through Full Achievement. Eventually, seven other Jesuit Scholastics joined him. They all slept in bunk beds in one room.

One night, as he was lying in bed, Paul looked out the window at an expanse of rooftops and chimneys. "It looked like a British or Irish city with all the chimneys," he recalls. "And it dawned on me that it looked great at the top, but if you looked down, at the bottom, reality—crime, poverty, drugs, alcohol, violence, despair—set in."

Paul spent his two summers at Boys Town, studying how that organization, founded in 1917 by the legendary Father Flanagan, operated. When he was finally ordained to the priesthood, he came back to St. Louis to start his life's work.

Instead of building one large facility like Boys Town that would bring children in from all over the country, Father Paul decided to house a small group of students in a residential home near a Catholic school. The home would be run by houseparents, and college-educated volunteers would help. He would call it Boys Hope.

The first house opened with three boys in St. Louis in 1976. It was an old two-family home that was totally refurbished by volunteers from St. Louis University. That was the start.

In 1979 he opened two homes in Chicago and two more in New York. A year later, Boys Hope spread to New Orleans. Then there was a seven-year gap during which Father Paul tracked down funding before he opened four more homes, in Ohio, Michigan, and Pennsylvania. In 1990 he expanded to Brazil and Guatemala. By 1998 Boys Hope had become Boys Hope Girls Hope, and there were thirty homes in seventeen cities, including one in Ireland.

Children are referred to Boys Hope Girls Hope by a variety of agencies. Screening for the program focuses on identifying the kids who have the greatest need and also have the potential to turn themselves around with the help of the program. There is no typical kid; what they have in common is that they all have suffered.

Boys Hope Girls Hope is truly saving people, one life at a time. And while the rewards are great, getting the program to where it is today was not easy. Father Paul remembers a time when he didn't know how he was going to get funding to keep the program going.

"I remember one night after the fourth year of operations," he says. "We had no money. I was so worried, I threw up. How were we going to take care of these kids? How was I going to keep from embarrassing our national board?"

That night, Father Paul turned again to God. "I said, 'Lord, I'm not trusting You enough. I promise I won't ever again *not* trust You. I'll do what I can do and let You do the rest.'

"It worked."

He found the strength to continue to beat the bushes

for funding, and the money eventually came. Not that it was easy, he says, but the job got done.

He had discovered another truth of life: if you believe in what you are doing and follow your calling, the answers will present themselves. It's a funny thing. For those who do not have faith in their own mission, lack of money can be an insurmountable obstacle. For those who believe, it is merely a hurdle. It may be difficult to get over, but it can be conquered. It comes down to what you put first. If you make the money the most important thing, it will consume you and what you are doing. If you put your mission first, the money will be there.

Once Father Paul trusted God, his mind was clear to do what he had to do to keep the program running. For two decades it grew and became strong.

After twenty years, Father Paul's superiors summoned him and told him that they wanted him to take another assignment, to give Boys Hope Girls Hope to someone else.

"If they were ever going to give me another job, they had better do it then, before I was old enough to retire," he says. "An organization ultimately has to live on its own. If it is to last and survive, it can't be identified with one person. It has to be bigger than the person running it."

Father Paul thought about it and agreed with his superiors. He asked for two more years to get everything in order and to oversee the transition. The new head of Boys Hope Girls Hope, John Dolman, a layman, took over in 1998, and Father Paul was assigned to be the president of the Jesuits' high school in St. Louis, where he could remain close to his kids.

Letting go was difficult, he admits. But his vow of obedience and his confidence that he had done everything possible in his final two years to put the program on a firm financial and organizational footing helped him to make the transition.

He spent his last summer with the program at a summer camp on a lake in Canada that Boys Hope Girls Hope had owned for years. There he got to know kids from all the cities, to talk to them about their dreams and ambitions.

One boy in particular moved him that summer. "He was from the bayous in Louisiana," Father Paul says, "and I asked him why he was there.

"He said, 'I've been tortured and beaten by my mother and father. They tied me to a chair naked for days at a time. They burned me with cigarettes.' He pulled up his shirt and showed me the scars all over his body. He said that finally he was left homeless. 'My mom jumped off a bridge and killed herself one day. My dad was arrested for selling drugs.'

"I started crying, which I've never done," Father Paul says. "The boy was between the seventh and eighth grades, and he saw me crying. He tapped me on the thigh and said, 'Father, why are you crying?'

" 'Because of what happened to you,' Father Paul said.

" 'You know what happened when I was tied up and tortured?' the boy replied.

" 'Yeah,' Father Paul said. 'You hurt.'

" 'No,' the boy said. 'I found my best friend—God. When I was tied up for days, I started to pray.' "

Father Paul was moved to the bottom of his soul by the

boy's story. And his amazement grew exponentially at what the boy said next.

" 'By the way, Father, don't you think I'm blessed?'

" 'How?' Father Paul asked.

" 'Didn't I find out who my best friend is—God? And didn't you give me a home?' "

The boy was completely sincere. He felt that all his suffering had led him to something wonderful. And when Father Paul thought about it, he realized the boy was right.

"That was the affirmation," he says quietly.

By being aware and open to a Moment of Truth, Father Paul Sheridan was able to give himself—and many others—a gift beyond all price.

ANNE MEAGHER NORTHUP

If Anne Meagher Northup had put her own needs first, she would be working nine to five in an office, just another anonymous worker in corporate America. Instead, she thought of what she could do not just for herself but for her city, her state, and her country. At the time, she had no idea where her path would lead, just that she wanted to be in public service. The fact that it led to Congress is not the point. That she listened to her heart when she arrived at her Moment of Truth is everything.

She is a two-term congresswoman, a Republican from a solidly Democratic district in Louisville, Kentucky, who fights hard for education and health-care reform, a woman who has been on *Larry King Live*, *Hardball with Chris Matthews*, *Meet the Press*, and other major television shows.

Meet Anne Meagher Northup, the Brownie leader and

PTA president who went to Congress, the woman who grew up with nine sisters and one brother in a home where being able to play flag football was a social skill more important than looking pretty in a frilly dress.

"It wasn't a woman's world in our house," she says. "We were all very athletic, very competitive. My dad organized the fall flag football games. The other neighbors asked to participate, but we were the quarterbacks. We climbed trees the highest. We always wanted to be better than everyone else. Anytime you wanted, you could run into the house and come out with two kickball teams.

"I'm more a product of my upbringing than anything else," Anne says. "Being one of eleven kids with very disciplined, very bright, very hardworking parents. Very driven parents. My parents were dedicated to making a difference every day of their lives and trusting in the Lord.

"When I speak to kids today, I tell them, 'Don't be afraid to live your life and take a chance. Don't be afraid to fail.' "

Anne attended St. Mary's College, the women's school across the street from the University of Notre Dame in South Bend, Indiana, and married Robert Wood "Woody" Northup. Even then, she much preferred talking politics and public policy than discussing Notre Dame football. That's something that has been with her all her life.

"In high school, I dated people who had characteristics in common—a star football player, the state wrestling champion," she says. "But what I remember about high school is everybody sitting in the drive-in, goofing around, drinking Cokes, and I'd say, 'Did everybody see that article on the editorial page today?'

"I had a fun side," she laughs, "but I could sustain it only so long. I always had a compelling interest in current events and politics and not enough hours in the day to indulge it."

Thirty years ago that was the rule for women. Even though there are more opportunities for women today, most can identify with Anne's dilemma. With a disproportionate share of housework and child care still falling to women, there is never enough time. The easiest path to follow is usually that dictated by society. But for Anne, who knew how to hear a Moment of Truth, it wasn't a matter of taking the easy path, but the one she knew was right.

Anne learned early about the realities of the American workplace for women. Upon graduating from college with a B.A. in economics and business, she got a job in her hometown of Louisville with a major corporation. The office in which she worked was an all-male bastion that was in the process of integrating its workforce with women. When she signed on, "They didn't even have female secretaries," she says. "It didn't take one week to figure out that the way to get ahead didn't depend on using my brains. The men wanted to flirt. They wanted to tell dirty jokes."

When the men told her such jokes, she said to them, "Would you tell that to your daughter?" They rolled their eyes and replied, "How square."

Change happens only when people have the courage to do what is right, even if it means being called names. Because of such pioneers as Anne, who had the courage of their convictions, the workplace eventually would be protected against such offensive behavior by antiharassment laws. Anne had no way of knowing then, but nearly thirty years later, her experiences would become painfully relevant to the nation when President Clinton was first accused of having an affair with a White House intern. Anne spoke out on the president's behavior, wondering as she did why nearly all of her female colleagues kept silent during the long impeachment proceedings.

"I've been in a workplace like this before," she told a reporter for *Salon*, the on-line magazine, "where a guy who had all the power was constantly after young, provocatively dressed women. And what it does to a workplace is profound. What it says is that having that swagger and that wink is what makes a real man. It puts pressure on other men to behave the same way.

"In the end, the guy with all the power loses moral authority over the entire organization, and everyone feels there are no rules."

As for the women, she went on, "They all get the feeling that their careers depend on being coy and seductive rather than on working hard and bringing their talents to the workplace. And it always ends up affecting the powerless person. But most important are all the other women whose jobs are affected—the secretary who has to cover, who has to lie to the wife. Everybody else has to become an enabler, and it affects their jobs, too."

She was almost alone during the impeachment debate, one of the few women talking about the real issue—the treatment of women in the workplace—instead of the political issues—should the president be impeached? Standing alone has been a hallmark of Anne's life.

It began with that first corporate job, which she left to

take a position as a teacher. She taught for two years, then resigned to become a full-time mother. She and Woody had two children, David and Katie. She wanted a big family, and when it looked for a time as if she would have no more children of her own, she and Woody adopted an African-American child from the inner city, Joshua.

"I had volunteered for Catholic Charities," she says, "and I knew there are children who have nobody in line to adopt them. We wanted another baby. We didn't even think about what color the baby was."

She doesn't consider that adoption to be a Moment of Truth. Yet, for most people, it would have been a difficult choice. Think about it. You are a middle-class person in the South, and you adopt a child of color. It takes a special kind of person to dive into a decision like that without a thought as to what others will think and say. Anne is that special person who believes she can help herself most by helping others.

Anne then gave birth to Kevin, adopted another African American, Erin, and finally had her last child with Woody, Mark, ten years after the birth of their first child in 1971.

She became the consummate mother, taking her kids to sports practices, becoming a Brownie leader, joining the PTA, volunteering for all sorts of charities. The thought of getting into politics was the farthest thing from her mind. There was, after all, never enough time.

Then, in 1985, her husband's company dissolved the division he worked for, which made sound systems for motorcycles, and Woody decided to buy out the division and run it himself. They went deeply into debt to finance the new company, and Anne soon saw that she would have to go back to work to help make ends meet.

"Mark was three and a half and going into nursery school," she says. "I didn't want to go back to teaching. I asked myself what would make me get up at five thirty in the morning to fold the clothes so I could get out at nine and go to work. What kind of job would be so challenging, so compelling, that I would make that sacrifice?

"There was no question—I love public policy."

She didn't think of it that way at the time, but it was Anne's Moment of Truth. She knew she had to get a job, and she could get one that simply earned money, or she could do what she had always wanted to do, but never thought she could. She could help herself or help others. She went with her heart, and there was no agony in the decision, only ecstasy.

She approached Mitch McConnell, her state senator. "Where do I start?" she asked. She was directed to the minority office in the Democrat-controlled Kentucky House of Representatives and given a job in the minority whip's office in the state legislature. "I was doing what an intern would do, but I was too old to be an intern," she says.

The pay wasn't anything—just $250 a week for the twelve weeks every other year that the state legislature was in session. But Anne was in heaven. "From the first day, I knew my life had changed. To actually read the newspaper every morning, then have the privilege to drive in my car to Frankfort [the state capital] and evaluate the chances of passage of the bills in front of the legislature . . . it gave me a sense of purpose. I didn't have to think about it for five minutes."

That was in 1986. A year later, Fred Cowan, the state representative in her district, which included the inner city of Louisville, ran in the spring primary for state attorney general. Anne remembers being at the pool with her friends, trying to teach her youngest, Mark, how to put his head underwater. "If Fred wins the primary," she told her friends, "I think I'm going to run for his seat."

"You're going to do what?!" she heard back.

She repeated her idea, and someone asked, "Who appointed you to do that?"

"Democracy," she replied. "If you want to run, all you have to do is fill out a form, pay twenty dollars, and run. Then you let the voters decide."

The women in her group were all involved in the community in one way or another, and they frequently sat around a table during swim team practices arguing about public policy. The more they thought about it, the more they liked Anne's decision and the more they supported her. "They've been great about it," she says.

The biggest mental hurdle to overcome was the natural question that everyone who goes into public service must ask—what did she have to offer? "I decided that I probably could make a contribution," she says. "And I probably did have some ideas. My terrible fear was that all these people would be around me and what would I have to say? I found I did have something to offer."

When Cowan won his primary, Anne filed her papers. In a way, she was lucky that the district she wanted to represent was heavily Democratic, as was the state House of Representatives, so the Republicans were glad to have anyone who was willing to campaign in a race that seemed a guaranteed loser.

For the next five months, Anne walked door-to-door in her district, through hundred-degree heat and ninety-eight percent humidity, through rain and whatever the weather had to throw at her, introducing herself by saying, "I want to run for the state House."

"I loved it," she says.

And, against all odds, this complete newcomer, a Republican in a Democratic district, won. So she went to Frankfort as a state representative. The pay still wasn't much—$500 a month for the twelve weeks the legislature was in session. "It wasn't even enough to pay my car phone bills," she admits. But she was hooked. At last she was in a position to do things to make people's lives better.

Others in politics worry about getting reelected. "The fear of losing drives their actions much more than the fear of doing the wrong thing," she says. "I'm driven to do the right thing. The best way our democracy works is if we all, in a straightforward way, put our ideas on the table and do what is best for the country."

By 1994 Anne was ready for a new challenge. "I had been in the state legislature for nine years. I'd been sitting in committee sessions hearing the same debates. People told me to run for mayor or judge, but I didn't want that. I really like the legislative process.

"Woody said, 'Why don't you run for Congress?'

"I said, 'I can't do that. I can't go to Washington.'

" 'Yes, you can,' Woody said. 'You'd be fabulous.'

"It was a very difficult decision for me," Anne says. She

would have to move to Washington and maintain another residence. It would take her away from her family for huge chunks of time. But her kids were growing up, Woody's business was finally in the black and doing well. Finally, she decided to give it a try.

Again, running as a Republican in a Democratic district, Anne won a narrow 1,300-vote victory in the 1996 general election. But Anne was not a prototypical Republican. She is a right-to-lifer, but she is also deeply committed to education reform. In the Kentucky legislature, she was one of only two Republicans who voted for education reform. She is also committed to health-care reform and to helping the residents of the inner cities end the poverty cycle.

She has had personal experience with many of her pet causes. She founded the House Reading Caucus in 1998, partly because she discovered she was mildly dyslexic and that had hindered her in school. Her knowledge of health care is deeply personal, as her daughter, Katie, has Hodgkin's disease and one of her sons was born with cerebral palsy.

"I know what happens when you don't attack learning disabilities early," she says. "Because of Katie, I learned a lot about protocols and what radiation does to you. I sit on the ethics board for sickle-cell anemia and I am on House boards and caucuses dealing with disabilities, diabetes, strokes and heart disease, and cancer awareness."

When she ran for reelection in 1998, she won by a slightly larger margin—four percentage points. She continues to do what she believes is right for the country, guided by her strong sense of morality. Following her conscience is more important to her than getting reelected.

"I could lose," she admits. But, she adds, "So what? I'm still going to be Woody's wife. I'm still going to be David, Katie, Joshua, Kevin, Erin, and Mark's mother."

Anne Meagher Northup is a rare politician who is motivated not by personal ambition but by a desire to serve the public. The country could use more like her.

MITCHELL S. ROSENTHAL

In the United States, where the individual is celebrated, we sometimes become self-absorbed and forget that we are part of many larger communities—our family, our neighborhood, our town, our country, and the world. As a result, we often miss the greater happiness and satisfaction that lie in being part of something greater than ourselves. Mitch Rosenthal's Moment of Truth came when he opened himself up to that larger community. His life is a wonderful example of how rich the rewards can be when we put others first.

Maybe, like Mitchell S. Rosenthal, you have to grow up, as he puts it, "pathologically private" to build something as vehemently open as Phoenix House. Or maybe you just have to bring an open mind and a desire to help people change their lives. Either way, you may end up, like Mitch, changing your own life as well.

Mitch knew as a child that he wanted to be a psychiatrist. But he always thought he would be a Freudian analyst, dividing his workday into fifty-minute hours, working mostly with children in New York City, one at a time. That's how one did battle with life in his family, one on one.

"I grew up in a family so private we didn't even say that somebody had a cold," he says. That was in Brooklyn, and his childhood took place in the 1940s and early 1950s. He went to Lafayette College in Easton, Pennsylvania. The Korean War was in full swing, and all students had to join either the military reserves or the Reserve Officer Training Corps—R.O.T.C.

No one knew how long the war would last, and Mitch decided to join the Navy Reserve. That way, he could finish his studies before going off to war, and he wouldn't have to go as a second lieutenant in the Army, but as an officer in the Navy.

After graduating from Lafayette, he went to New York University Medical School in New York City. Then there was an internship and residency and a fellowship in child psychology. By the time he was ready for active duty, it was 1965. He was thirty years old and married, and he already had a small, private practice in child psychology.

Mitch expected the Navy to assign him to the local military hospital in St. Albans, Queens. He would continue his private practice on the side, and when he had completed his active duty requirement in two years, he would be in New York, his home, ready for the rest of his professional life.

Mitch was about to discover that sometimes life has other plans for us. Instead of keeping him in New York, the Navy sent him to the San Francisco Bay Area, where they needed someone to teach child psychiatry to other Navy doctors at Oak Knoll Hospital in Oakland. But when Mitch got to Oakland, the Navy's priorities changed. The Vietnam war was expanding, and with draftees filling the ranks of the military services, increasing numbers of young men were being declared, as the Navy put it, "problem children."

"These were the kids who didn't conform to military life," Mitch says. "They were constantly getting into trouble, getting arrested, drinking, kiting checks, doing drugs. These were kids who had trouble in high school, kids who had trouble with their families. They had not suddenly erupted into bad behavior. They came to the Navy with problems."

There were two ways to get rid of such problem kids. The first was for their line officers to reject them as unfit for service. But if an officer rejected a number of sailors, it reflected poorly on him as a leader and could affect his career. The alternative was to send them to a naval psychiatric unit and have a psychiatrist declare them unfit for duty, a finding that led to a recruit's being discharged or, in military parlance, "sectioned out."

That kind of medical discharge stays with you forever, labeling you as someone who is unstable. If you were unfit for duty in the military, employers tended to assume you would be unfit for them as well. "To me, it seemed to be an awful mistake to just stamp them unfit for duty rather than being constructive and doing something to change their lives," Mitch says. Such a discharge "confirms your own notion of yourself as a failure and someone who's never been able to make it. These people see themselves as chronic failures. They fail in their family life. They fail in school. They fail at work. And now they were failing in the military."

The Navy had a war to fight, and if you couldn't follow orders and be trustworthy and dependable, the military couldn't use you.

The commanders saw numbers. But Mitch saw the real people who made up those numbers. If he could find a way to rescue some of these "problem children," he would be saving not only lives, but also—and this would make the Navy happy—he would be saving all the money that had been invested in training them.

One thing was clear. Traditional, one-on-one psychotherapy was not the answer. There were neither therapists enough nor time enough for that lengthy process.

An idea came to Mitch prepackaged and unexpected. Being young and eager to learn, he had begun exploring the opportunities around him in his free time. He learned that two recovering drug addicts were scheduled to speak about their experiences with an organization called Synanon in San Francisco. Curiosity led him there. At the time, Synanon was a new and vibrant program that used intensive group encounters to help people labeled losers turn their lives around.

"It was almost exclusively for people with serious drug problems," Mitch says. "Many of them had prison histories as well. In my own training I had worked with people with alcohol and drug problems, and when I heard these two people speak, I was very taken with what a remarkable change had occurred in their lives.

"I began to study what they were doing at Synanon, and I felt that a lot of it could be modified and translated to work in other settings."

To better study the dynamic of the Synanon group encounter, Mitch joined the group himself.

"I was very taken with how powerful this group technique was," he says. "You have twelve to fifteen people sitting in a circle and trying to focus their energies on having a single individual look at himself. They were mirroring back behaviors and attitudes that most of us take for granted most of the time.

"When a dozen people start to talk to you about being late, or about how you spoke to them, when people start to give you little vignettes of yourself back, it is enormously powerful."

In traditional psychotherapy, he says, "you're with the patient for only an hour. But in a therapeutic community, you have many observers, not just one, and it's not going on for just a fifty-minute hour, but, as they say now, 24/7—twenty-four hours a day, seven days a week. If you're sitting in a room with people who come to know you because you sleep in the same dorm, work in the same kitchen, do the same things they do, they are your working companions and your family, as well. If they don't function well, it affects you.

"For me, it became, if not a Moment of Truth, a Period of Truth, where I refocused my professional energies. As someone trained in very individual techniques, I began to see that we had a new kind of social psychiatry that would allow you to use peer relationships so that we had mutual help and self-help that was far more powerful in helping people see themselves than conventional psychotherapy."

The change this experience wrought in Mitch could not have been more profound. "This was a radical departure," he says. "I was a member of the group, so the group could talk to me and tell me how they saw me, and I could talk to them. For somebody who grew up in a family that was so private, to be so publicly open and sharing was mind-boggling.

"It was frightening," he goes on. "And yet, in another way, it was freeing. At some point, you say, 'It doesn't matter that I held on to all these little secrets I thought were so precious. I thought they were so unique, and they're not unique.' It's a very liberating experience to find yourself connected with a group of people who become your buddies, because you have shared fundamental truths about your life. It's a fundamentally reassuring experience.

"As you go deeper into the human drama of their family lives, you find out that rich, poor, black, white, in different ways all have suffered family traumas."

Even as a doctor trained to see the common elements among all people, Mitch found this interaction personally awakening. This growing realization was emphasized by the disintegration of Mitch's first marriage and by his own sense of loss and failure. "Looking at my own sadness and depression was part of that," he says. "I would have gotten over the pain of divorce anyway, but what the encounter group did on another level was open me to examining my-self and sharing with others in a very personal way. That strengthened me enormously." Before he knew it, he was curing himself of what he calls pathological privacy.

He proposed to his superiors in the Navy that he start a six-month pilot program at Oak Knoll to see, as he says, "if by using intensive group therapy techniques with these kids, we could return men to active duty."

He began with fifty sailors and marines, all patients in that section of the hospital traditionally known in the mili-tary as "squirrel hill," because everyone there was nuts. Through the dynamic of the group, the patients started be-having in decidedly unsquirrelly ways. "Instead of everyone walking around in their pajamas, they started wearing their uniforms, pressed and creased," Mitch says. Rather than looking like the rejects that they were supposed to be, they began to look like the best the Navy offered.

"They were getting feedback, and it wasn't just that someone didn't like what they did, but it was what they saw you doing. It gave them ways to become accountable for their behavior that they didn't have before.

"These people are very destructive to all the people they cherish and value, and especially to themselves," he goes on. "But until they became members of the group, they never recognized their own behavior."

At one time in their lives peer pressure had reinforced their self-destructive behavior. Now peer pressure was free-ing and healing them.

America treasures the rugged individual, but that's largely a fiction of Hollywood. In the real world, we rely, for good or ill, on those around us, as they rely on us. When Mitch started out in life, he thought of himself as the individual, running his own practice, one doctor and one patient at a time. He would have been successful. But he would not have had the impact he has had by taking a very different course. Once he stopped thinking of himself, he was free to help others.

The Navy Command took notice. "They always looked at people who had psychological problems as people willfully not participating or goofing off or, to use another military term, being dishonorable," Mitch says. "Now, to have the behavior come to a level of high performance and honor and accountability was very startling. And our success won us a lot of support to keep the project going."

Of the fifty people in the group, Mitch and his fellow psychiatrists were able to return seventy percent to active duty. In a results-oriented society, those were results of the highest order.

When Mitch finished his two years of active duty, he was transformed. "I gave up traditional practice," he says. "I dedicated my whole professional life to this type of work."

In the process, he had found the beginnings of true fulfillment.

In 1967 he took what he learned back to New York, where he became deputy commissioner for rehabilitation for the city. At that time heroin was "the drug everyone was afraid of, the drug driving the crime problem," Mitch says.

The government dedicated millions of dollars to fighting the problem, and Mitch used some of it to found his treatment facility, which he named Phoenix House after the mythological bird that is consumed by fire and rises again from its own ashes. Begun as a government program, Phoenix House was restructured after three years as a private, not-for-profit foundation.

Since then, the drug of choice has changed many times, but the reality of addiction has not. Nor has the effectiveness of the group-encounter rehabilitation program. It takes time—a year or more—but it produces results, and it has changed tens of thousands of lives for the better.

During all that time Mitch has remained true to the commitment he made as a young Navy psychiatrist. He has written numerous books and articles, consulted with similar programs around the world, and continued to expand Phoenix House until, at the end of 1999, his program was operating some seventy programs in eight states for five thousand people, both children and adults.

The people he helps fight the same battles he first encountered at Synanon in San Francisco. "Whether they're seventeen years old or thirty-five years old," he says, "they see themselves as chronic failures. They think they're never going to make it."

At Phoenix House, thanks in large part to Mitchell S. Rosenthal, they learn they *can* make it.

HENRY AND PATRICIA KING

I know of few people as selfless as Patricia and Henry King. The couple adopted a child from Honduras and the experience was so trying that they vowed never to return to that country again. Yet when the opportunity came for them to adopt another child, they realized that what they had thought was a difficult trial was an enormous blessing—and their Moment of Truth. Rather than turn their backs on a land in desperate need of help, the Kings threw themselves into creating hope and opportunity where none had existed.

She was a single woman of thirty-one, a tennis instructor and an actress in a local amateur theater group, living comfortably enough in the genteel and wealthy Jersey Shore community of Spring Lake, where she had grown up.

He was fifty-nine and also single, a busy executive, a

devout Catholic widower with fifteen children, only one of whom, a fifteen-year-old girl, was still at home.

Her name was Patricia Poe, and she was tall and blond and blue-eyed. His was Henry King, and he was witty and engaging, a man who had traveled the world and counted among his friends the rich and the powerful.

They met at rehearsals for a play in which she and Henry's youngest daughter, Margaret, had parts. Neither Henry nor Patricia had any intention of falling in love. "I never thought about getting married again," says Henry, whose first wife, Ottilie Sandrock, the mother of all his children, had died of cancer.

But they met and they talked and they fell in love.

"He was the most interesting man I ever met," says Patricia.

"I sold her a bill of goods," laughs Henry.

Maybe the play had something to do with it. Its title, Patricia says with an infectious laugh, was *Anything Goes.* "How prophetic is that?" she asks.

The romance set tongues to wagging in the insular little community. He was, after all, older than her mother. Even Henry's children weren't thrilled. But the old monsignor in their parish settled things down. When someone came to him to ask how he could bless such a May–November union, he fibbed and said, "I introduced them."

Henry and Patricia married in 1980, and after a couple of years Pat suddenly realized, "I wanted to have children of my own." Even though Henry was finally getting his last child through college, he agreed to start all over again.

But Pat had had medical problems and found she couldn't get pregnant. Undeterred, they decided to adopt.

For more than a year, they went to dozens of adoption agencies, and every one gave them the same answer, which boiled down to "sorry." Some said Henry was too old. His own Catholic diocese of Trenton, New Jersey, told him, "You have enough children. You don't need any more."

They tried to adopt a Korean baby, but the law in that country held that there could not be more than a forty-year difference in age between the oldest adoptive parent and the child being adopted. That limited the Kings to a "child" of twenty. They tried Ireland and the Philippines. No luck. Only Jerry Falwell, the born-again leader of the Christian Right, was willing to listen to them. He said they could have a baby, but they had to raise it as a born-again Christian. The Kings, both devout Catholics, thanked him sincerely but couldn't agree to that.

The longer their search went on, the more depressed Pat got. After nearly four years of fruitless effort, she was ready to give up. Then, one day, at a cocktail party thrown by the United States Brewers Association, of which Henry had been president, they told a friend about their disheartening experience. The friend told them about a mission in Honduras that might have a child for them.

It was like a lifeline thrown to a drowning woman. Pat wanted a child so badly, if someone had told her she could get one at the South Pole, she would have gone there immediately. There is no explaining it other than that the need to have children is as ancient as life itself. Another woman, confronting similar obstacles, might have given up. For many, the thought of raising a child of a different ethnic background would have been too daunting.

This opportunity became a test of Pat's desire to have a child. Would she travel a thousand miles to a country she couldn't find on the map to fulfill her quest?

The answer was clear to her. She would continue the journey she had started, even if she had no idea where it would take her.

She wrote a letter to the head of the Honduran mission, Sister Teresita Gonzalez of the School Sisters of Notre Dame, a teaching order of Catholic nuns. Tere, as the Kings have come to call her, receives more than a hundred letters annually inquiring after the twelve or fifteen babies that she finds homes for each year. Most, she doesn't even answer.

"I don't know what it was about our letter, but she wrote us back," says Pat. After more letters and phone calls and credential checks, Tere agreed to give them a baby when one became available.

In May 1986 Tere called the Kings and told them she had to go to Mexico for several months and would not be back in Honduras until January. They should not expect to hear from her before then. The Kings put their revived hopes on hold and went about their lives. Then, at 11:30 P.M. on October 2, Tere called. "I have a baby. He's yours," she said.

"We weren't expecting to hear from her until January," Pat says. "We didn't know what to do."

There were papers and forms to get from what seemed like everywhere—the Immigration and Naturalization Service, the State Department, the Honduran Government, and on and on; sixty-three pages in all, and each one had to be signed and stamped and sealed. It took four weeks to get all the paperwork done, and all the while Tere was calling, asking when they were going to come down for the baby.

With the sheaf of documents in hand, the Kings flew to Tegucigalpa, the capital of Honduras. They were met at the airport by a representative of Tere and taken to a hotel. There, a woman handed Pat a month-old baby boy and said, *"Es suyo"*—"He's yours."

They named the boy Andrew, but they were not home free. There remained documents and approvals to obtain in Honduras, where the bureaucracy is as inept and corrupt as anywhere in the world. Henry returned to the States to attend to his business, and Pat checked into a hotel in Tegucigalpa with Andrew to fight her way through the bureaucrats.

"I thought we'd be home by Thanksgiving," she says. "I was there until Easter."

Pat was used to being surrounded by friends and family, but here she knew no one. She learned the language, made the daily rounds of government offices, took her baby for long walks, and began to absorb the culture that had given birth to her son and what it meant to be a mother.

In retrospect, it was a blessing, a daily succession of Moments of Truth that prepared her for what was to come. If she had been given her baby and left the next day, that might have been the end of it. But the long stay was an education that would change the way she viewed life and the world.

Tere's convent was thirty miles away, and for the first two months Pat lived alone. "I'd be stepping over homeless people in the streets," she says. "I would see children with children of their own." She was getting her first look at life in the dirt-poor Third World.

When she asked why it was taking so long to complete the adoption, an official told her, "We have to be careful about what happens to our children." It was all she could do to keep from screaming at the man and asking him exactly how much he cared about all the dirty and half-starved kids in the streets, about the ten-year-old girls having babies, the eight-year-olds being sold by their own mothers to houses of prostitution.

On Christmas, Henry returned with a tiny Christmas tree, complete with lights, that he bought at the airport. He unfolded it in the hotel room and plugged it in. "It was pathetic," Pat says, laughing at the memory.

When Henry went back to New Jersey, Pat accepted Tere's invitation to live in the convent until she finally got clear of all the red tape.

At the convent, Pat finally was around people who cared about her. She had other women to talk to, things to do. She was also getting a deeper lesson about the realities of life in that godforsaken little country.

People were constantly knocking on the door, looking for the simplest of things. "An old homeless man came in in a lot of pain. He wanted one aspirin," Pat says, still profoundly shocked at a country in which an aspirin tablet is a rare and precious commodity. "A fourteen-year-old girl came by. She had sold herself to a man for five dollars and now she was pregnant. She wanted help."

Day after day, Pat witnessed the heartbreaking procession. There was "Little Onion," a boy not yet six whose father brought him down to the main square of town every day and chained him to a park bench with a box of onions for him to sell. Then the man went out and got drunk, sometimes leaving the boy chained to the bench all night.

Another time, she saw a mother taking her eight-year-old girl into a bar to sell her for what little money she could get. Pat asked the woman how she could do such a thing, and her reply pierced Pat's heart: "Life stinks. She may as well learn that now."

"I don't know how they could even answer the door," Pat says of the nuns. "I couldn't."

She was there for two months, and the experience touched her more deeply and permanently than she knew at the time. "I realize now those two months were my Moment of Truth," Pat says. "I have never looked at anything the same way again."

Pat had grown up in relative affluence. Her sense of poverty was not being able to afford cable television. She returned to New Jersey with an entirely new concept of the necessities of life. She had seen people with literally nothing but the rags on their backs, living in the most awful circumstances imaginable.

"I never realized how tough people are," she says. "I didn't know how tough babies are."

At the time, though, she had no idea how those months in Honduras would affect her. When she finally got the last paper signed and left Honduras with Andrew, "I had no intention of ever going back."

But time is a great healer. Like the pain of real childbirth, Pat's trials receded from her memory, and she thought only of how much joy Andrew had brought into her life. So when Tere called again to say she had another young girl who was pregnant and wanted to give her baby up for adoption, Pat and Henry readily agreed to take her child.

Their second son, Tim, was born in 1988. This time, Pat went to Honduras knowing that she would return again and again and again.

"When I went down for Tim, it all came together," Pat says. She had been raised to be charitable, but where she grew up, charity was as much a social event as a moral obligation. Her Moment of Truth had allowed her to see that true charity isn't always fashionable and doesn't necessarily come with a cocktail party. In Honduras there were people for whom no one seemed to care, desperate for the simplest necessities of life.

She stopped at the convent to see Tere. The nuns there were ecstatic because they had just raised some money for an orphanage they wanted to build. Pat asked them how much money they needed. "Sixty thousand dollars," Tere said. How much had they raised? "A couple hundred."

At that rate it would be a generation before the orphanage was a reality. Pat promised to get the money.

"You see what needs to be done, and you do it. This was a way we could give something back," says Pat.

"Don't worry," she told Tere. "Henry has a lot of rich friends."

When she got home, she told Henry that she had promised to build the orphanage. Instead of going to his rich friends, Henry went to the local bank and took out a mortgage on his house for the $60,000. "What if I die?" he asked Pat. "How will we pay it back?"

"Don't worry," she said. "God will provide."

Henry wasn't sure that God would come down with a check if he cashed in his chips, but he went ahead anyway.

They raised more money, and Pat went to classes at her local Home Depot to learn about construction. When all was ready in 1990, she rounded up twenty high school kids who volunteered to pay their own way to Honduras. Once there, they made their own cinder blocks and built a home and classrooms for fifty boys. They called it Hogar Amistad—House of Friendship.

Within a year, Pat was back in Honduras, building a second orphanage and a school for fifty girls. Then they bought a farm, where they housed still more orphans and taught the local peasants, who still practiced slash-and-burn agriculture, how to plow and plant and feed themselves using modern farming methods.

Each time the Kings went back to Honduras, they were struck by the lack of the most basic medical and dental care for the peasants. Tere told them it was even worse in the mountains, where there was no electricity, no sanitation, no knowledge of basic nutrition.

Thus was born another project for the Kings' growing Honduran charity. In addition to building, they began recruiting doctors and dentists along with their usual score of high school volunteers. Henry used his connections to get hundreds of pounds of donated medicines. In twelve days over the Easter holidays, they cared for four thousand people in the remote mountains.

Seeing the desperate need for year-round medical care, they raised money for and built a clinic in the isolated town of Urraco. Now, when they make their annual medical pilgrimage with some $200,000 worth of donated medicine, they have a headquarters from which to operate. And they have arranged to staff the clinic year-round.

Back home, people sometimes ask the Kings why they spend their time and money in Honduras when they could help people closer to home. Not one given to tact, Henry replies, "That's your job."

Pat and Henry have found they can do so much more with a dollar in Honduras than they can in the United States. For $75,000 a year, they can house and educate one hundred fifty children and give them a very real chance to lead productive lives. "For that, I couldn't even send six American kids to the local elementary school," Henry says.

Besides, Honduras gave them two fine sons, and even though the experience was the most difficult of their lives, they want to give something back. In their hearts, they are Honduran-Americans, and they have a debt to pay.

At the turn of the century, their first group of orphans is growing up and entering the skilled trades, where they can help to build a future for a country that has known little but misery. The second crop of orphans has started kindergarten, and the Kings expect most of them to go to college and become leaders of the next Honduran generation. Pat and Henry have also established the House of Friendship Foundation in Bel Mar, New Jersey, where they now live, so that funds will be available to keep their dream alive after they are gone.

Henry turned seventy-nine in the year 2000, but he says that his two sons and the work in Honduras have kept him young.

Pat never goes a day without thinking about the poor girls who gave up their babies for adoption to a couple from New Jersey. "It's such a beautiful gift," she says. "It's like a miracle."

It is a Moment of Truth.

PART TWO

Daily Struggles Often Bring Moments of Truth

*A*t some point, for just about everyone, life is a struggle. *But for some of us, the struggle is so constant that it takes over our lives until all we know is the age-old battle simply to make it through another day. At such times we don't have the luxury of thinking decisions through carefully or of setting long-term goals. We simply do what we have to do to feed our families and pay the rent.*

Yet out of that struggle great things can come if we remain open to the power of the Moments of Truth we encounter along the way. It is only later, when the battle is over and we find ourselves in the Promised Land, that we have the time to look back and see how it happened. If we look closely, we find that we succeeded because we sensed those Moments of Truth and acted on them.

Jack Fuller is an example of the amazing things that people can do when the struggle forces them to use every bit of their intelligence and creativity. Leveled by polio as a young adult, and told by his doctors that he would never get out of a wheelchair, he invented a way to walk.

Ann Liguori found herself young and jobless in the most unforgiving city of them all—New York. Her future was condensed into a single Moment of Truth when she had to convince an executive that she was worth his sponsorship. The result is America's longest-running sports interview show hosted by a woman.

You may not know Bernard Marcus, but you undoubtedly know his business—Home Depot. Based on one of the most successful marketing ideas of our era, it was born not so much out of careful planning and market research as out of necessity after Bernard lost his job. Bernard knows now that his business empire became possible because of a Moment of Truth, when he realized that he had to stop looking back and start looking forward.

Then there is Julia Stewart, whose Moment of Truth came when she was just twelve years old and trapped in a traumatic home situation. She needed to do something—anything—to make her parents see that they were destroying not only each other but also their only child.

Finally, we will meet Stephen and Elizabeth Wampler, who both lost their jobs just as they were starting life together. The necessity of feeding and housing themselves led them to a Moment of Truth that gave birth to a new service industry.

Every one of these people arrived where he or she is today by responding to the necessity of mere survival. When their Moments of Truth came, they weren't looking years down the road but at the obstacles right in front of them.

JACK FULLER

*I've often marveled at how many wonderful, selfless peo-
ple grew up during the Great Depression. Despite the
hardships of that time, it produced the generation that
stormed the beaches of the Pacific and Europe and
Africa; the generation that worked so hard during the
fifties; the generation that laid the groundwork for the
prosperity and technological wonders that make up today's exciting world. Yes, the Depression destroyed lives,
and we don't want to experience anything like it again.
But the people who lived through it brought with them
habits of hard work, self-reliance, and helping others
that are remarkable in this, or any, age. Jack Fuller is
one of those people.*

Jack Fuller doesn't think he's ever done anything extraordinary, never faced a moment of darkness, never had to

choose between two paths in life. With such a man, the best course is simply to tell his story and let you be the judge.

The native optimism that made Jack's life successful wasn't a family trait. Born in 1920, he grew up in Denver, the second of two children of an alcoholic father and a God-fearing, long-suffering mother. His father wasn't a mean drunk, didn't come home and curse the fates and his family. "He drank and he passed out," is how Jack puts it. But he was still a drunk.

Jack's father, a newspaper editor by trade, would climb on the wagon and stay sober for a while, then fall off and disappear for days or weeks at a time, taking his insecurities and his demons with him inside a bottle until the bottle was empty and he was insensible. During the Depression, as Jack grew up, his father seldom had a job.

But Jack didn't think life was tough or times were hard. "My mom held the family together," he says. "Dad couldn't find work. He even tried shoveling sugar beets. He wrote poems to my mom about how he felt he wasn't helping her at all. They broke your heart."

As bad as it sounds, Jack says with complete sincerity, "I never felt the Depression. One year for Christmas I got a scooter and I thought it was heaven-sent. Another year my dad made me a pair of stilts and my grandmother knitted me a sweater. I felt really blessed."

He was born with an eagerness to work and a disposition that never saw the obstacles. His family set up a pop stand on a street corner in Denver. Jack begged for ice from an iceman to cool the glass bottles that he bought from a wholesaler. He and his brother sold pop for a nickel a bottle and made a penny on each sale.

"There was always a way to make money," he says.

He delivered *Liberty* magazine door-to-door, making a nickel per delivery. Wanting a bicycle but lacking the means to buy one, he convinced the owner of a shoe store and repair shop that he could expand the man's business by using a bicycle that the shop owner's grown son had left behind. Jack began delivering and picking up shoes for a nickel a pair.

He was a Boy Scout and then an Eagle Scout and he joined the YMCA, where he learned how to run an eight-by-five flatbed printing press that the Y owned. When the Y decided to get out of the printing business, he convinced the administrators to let him take the press home and pay for it with the proceeds from the jobs he'd do.

He rattles off the jobs he had, and they seem never to end. "I worked for a drugstore. Mowed lawns. I learned how to clean houses and I learned to run a sewing machine. I learned how to paper walls and paint. I worked for a florist. I picked up a lot of crazy little skills.

"It was fun to do things. And there were always things to do, always jobs to be done. Always a way to make a little money."

That was the blessing of the Depression. When no one had anything, you didn't dwell on what you lacked. It wasn't as if the grass was greener on the other side of the fence. Chances were it was just as brown as it was in your yard. Envy and covetousness were rare, and there was no such thing as keeping up with the Joneses. It was more a case of doing what you could to live and every little extra thing you got—an afternoon at the movies, a cold bottle of Coke, a cupcake—was something to savor and enjoy. That's how Jack looked at it. It's how he looks at it still. He grew up tall and lanky—six two, 165 pounds—and took up swimming in high school. Along the way he was inspired by an electrical engineer who worked for General Electric, and he decided he would go to college, learn electrical engineering, and work for GE, too.

So off he went to the University of Colorado at Boulder, getting a room in a boardinghouse and paying his rent by polishing the hardwood floors with paste wax on his hands and knees. When General Electric sent a recruiter to campus to interview graduating seniors, Jack, just a freshman, got in line. "I didn't know it was only for seniors," he says. "I told the man I was going to work for General Electric and I wanted them to know who I was. Boy, was I naive."

He says it with a tinge of embarrassment—misplaced, in my opinion. Naivete is not a handicap if it makes you do something too early rather than not at all. Anyway, the recruiter didn't laugh at Jack or send him away. Instead, the man invited Jack to Lynn, Massachusetts, to work for the company during the summer. It was in Lynn, while attending church, that Jack met the woman who would become his wife—Jean.

That fall, he came back to Boulder and celebrated his twenty-first birthday. But he missed Jean so much he quit school and went back to Lynn, taking a full-time job with GE in product testing and enrolling at Massachusetts Institute of Technology. Meanwhile, he and Jean got married.

He was twenty-one and she was twenty-two, and even though World War II had just broken out, the world was at their fingertips.

Jack's charmed life didn't last. One day he noticed that his joints were sore and he felt sick. The illness didn't go away; instead it got worse and worse. It was rheumatic fever, a disease that attacked the joints and, in those days before antibiotics, had to run its course.

Even the months-long convalescence in bed was, to Jack, happy and fulfilling because, he says, "There were always things to read, projects to think about."

Jack never asked, "Why me?" Instead, he retained his unflagging belief that life is full of opportunities. Like the Depression, which offered him so many chances to learn so many jobs, his illness gave him the opportunity to improve his mind and to learn. Life, Jack Fuller was proving once more, is what you make of it.

By the time he recovered, he had contracted a heart murmur that prevented him from serving in the Army during the war. So he and Jean went back to Boulder, where he taught math and ran a repair shop for electrical appliances. After he got his bachelor's degree, in 1944, he went back to GE.

He has nothing but praise for the company, but what GE gave to Jack, he gave back, with interest. Whatever GE gave him to do, Jack dove into it. In return, the company kept giving him raises and, in his words, "treated me royally."

Others might have wanted even more from an employer, but Jack knew what he had in GE. What he didn't have didn't bother him. It's a good rule for all of us.

When the couple had been blessed with the first of their five children, an aunt that Jack didn't even know he had died in Michigan and left him two thousand dollars—a substantial amount of money in those days. The couple bought a house trailer with it and moved into the mountains. Then they traded the trailer for a cabin. Life was good.

But Jack came down with another fever, and this one didn't break. He got sicker and sicker until he could barely move. He was forced to go to the hospital, where he learned he had polio.

Few diseases were more feared at that time. Polio attacked the nerve fibers and killed them at random, destroying muscle tissue as well. Some people recovered with relatively minor damage, but many died, especially adult victims like Jack. Those who lived often suffered so much damage to muscles and nerves that they lost the ability to walk or even to move their limbs at all. There was no way to prevent the disease and no way to stop its progress.

All the doctors could do was move all polio patients into an isolation ward and feed them morphine to combat the excruciating cramping that would occur as the disease consumed nerves and muscles. When Jack went in, he says, "There was an epidemic, and six hundred people in Denver had polio.

"In the ward, no one could visit you," he adds. "The doctors told Jean that the only way she could visit was if I was about to die." One day, Jean got a call to come and visit her husband. She knew what that meant.

Confined to bed, unable to move, consumed by fever, Jack had lost 45 percent of his body mass and probably weighed no more than ninety pounds. "Jean said I looked like someone who had come out of a concentration camp," he says.

No longer conscious, he was hallucinating. "I felt like I was slipping," he says. "I walked down this long tunnel. At the end was a door with a big bright light. I got all the way down to the door and opened it. There was a figure there dressed in a brilliant white robe. Obviously, it was God."

The figure he met wouldn't let him through the door. "He said, 'You can't come yet, Jack. You have to go back.' "

Jack had always had a deep Christian faith, and he accepted what the figure told him. He turned around and started back. "I climbed all the way back up that long tunnel," he says. "It was really hard to get to the end." But he got there, and when he did, Jean was waiting at his bedside. Jack opened his eyes, looked at his wife, and said, "I'm in great shape. I'm not dying. I'm on my way back."

To me, that is a Moment of Truth as clear as a mountain spring. Jack was given not only his life but also a command. He had work to do, and God wanted him to do it. Jack sees it simply as the will of God in action, not something to question but something to accept. He understands what it can mean to others, and he says, "If it gives someone else inspiration, it's worth it."

He told me this story in 1999, more than fifty years after it happened, but the vision has never dimmed for him. "All I knew was that I had to stay on this side," he says. "My time hadn't arrived. I had to climb back up. It was a beautiful, white, shining area with a person in a white robe standing there. People hear about that and say, 'You were hallucinating.' But I was off the morphine. I was very aware of everything that was happening.

"I have a very strong faith," he goes on. "The good Lord said, 'Jack, you can't come yet.' I didn't know what plans He had for me. But I never had the slightest doubt that I would be able to go back to work and take care of my family. Even when I was totally paralyzed, I had no doubt. I wasn't hired because of what I could do with my body, but because of what I could do with my mind."

We live in a culture that celebrates the body, but Jack always knew that it is what is inside that body that truly determines who we are. He was lucky to have a woman who loved him as deeply as Jean did, and she was lucky to have a man who refused to feel sorry for himself.

He stayed in the hospital for five months, slowly regaining some mobility in his arms. As he lay in bed, he also began to solve problems again. One of the first was figuring out how to turn himself over in bed.

"It took three nurses to turn me over," he recalls. As he regained some strength in his arms, he hit on the idea of hooking up ropes and pulleys to an inverted traction frame above his bed. He had the nurses rig it up, and when it was done, not only could he turn himself, but he could pull the sheet back over his body. Soon, every traction frame in the hospital had been commandeered by the polio ward.

Jack then set his talents to helping a boy of sixteen who was so ravaged by polio he could barely move at all. Jack rigged spring-loaded props for the boy's arms and fashioned a spoon that wrapped around his hand. As the boy sat in his wheelchair, he was able to dip the spoon in the salad and the springs brought it back to his mouth.

"Tears streamed down his face," Jack remembers, choking up himself at the memory. "He said it was the best meal he had had since he entered the hospital. He was getting most of the salad in his mouth and some on his clothes. All of us had tears in our eyes."

Jack can't explain how he comes by his own optimism. He just knows that, even during those five months in the hospital and even when the doctors told him he would never walk again, he didn't ever feel depressed. For one thing, he knew he would walk again. For another, he knew he would go back to work and take care of his family. Finally, he was born a problem solver, and his confinement wasn't the end of anything. It was simply another problem to be solved.

All of us can learn from his approach to life. We might not be able to build contraptions to help people feed themselves, but we can always think of ways to get around the obstacles that life throws in our paths. And most of the obstacles that stop us are mental. Solving them is no different from solving the problems Jack encountered. It's just a matter of not quitting.

In order to move again, he had to retrain the muscles he had left. To do that, he first had to find out exactly which muscles still worked. He rigged an oscilloscope to an amplifier and two electrodes, which he jabbed into his muscles. When the muscles contracted, they generated an electrical impulse he could see on the oscilloscope. When Jack saw the blip on the screen, he concentrated on making that muscle move again. It was a long and painstaking process, but he slowly learned how to send signals to his muscles again.

He asked for a set of braces that would keep his legs straight while he used crutches to support his weight and move. He kept tinkering with the braces, making them work better and allowing them to take advantage of the muscles that still worked.

He never waited for somebody else to solve his problems for him. If technology hadn't yet caught up with his problem, he would help it along. His was the mind of an inventor at work.

When Jack finally got out of the hospital, he went back to work, ranging over a vast territory by car as a field engineer for General Electric, solving problems wherever he went. He never thought he was special for overcoming so many obstacles. Truth be told, he never really considered anything an obstacle.

"This is life," he explains. "My job was to get back and do the best job for GE that I could do and be the best husband I could be."

Jack always understood that he was able to do so much because he never stopped learning. He came to believe that, if we could educate our children as he had educated himself, we would all profit. He made education his mission, and he ran for the Denver school board, winning office on his second try and serving for six years. He was a pioneer in insisting on the development of a strong core curriculum. He was also an early champion of integration.

"I campaigned at all the fire stations. People would ask

me why I was running, and I said, 'It seems like it's important and I'd like to be of service. I am a child of life and I am here to serve.' "

In 1969 Jack's good friend, Bill Hannah, a professor at the University of Colorado, suggested that Jack become a teacher at the university. "Are you sure?" Jack asked. "I only have a bachelor's degree."

Hannah insisted that the lack of an advanced degree was not a hindrance. With many inventions to his name and a lifetime spent reading and learning, Jack was as qualified to teach electrical engineering as any Ph.D. was. Jack listened to what Bill had to say and was convinced. He so believed in the importance of education that he took a cut in pay to take the job. Yet, when he was offered a professorship with tenure before he had served the required time, he refused, insisting that he work his way into a tenured position like everyone else.

Today he would be called crazy for doing that. But Jack never grew out of the idea that life didn't owe him anything other than what he earned.

"I gave up the world's best job to take the world's best job," he says. "Most men don't have that opportunity."

He stayed at the university for twenty years, becoming cochairman of the engineering department—pretty good for a guy with only a bachelor's degree. But it shows that what's inside a man's head is more important than what's written on a diploma.

Jack retired at the age of sixty-nine, but he still wasn't done making a difference in the world. Over the years, he lost the ability to walk and became confined to an electric wheelchair. His vision deteriorated to the point where he was legally blind and could no longer drive.

In 1995 Jack started using Special Transit, a Boulder transportation service for senior citizens and the disabled. A year later, seeing a need for an expansion of the service, he raised $300,000 in nine months to renovate the operations center. "I thought it was time to pay back to the community for all the wonderful things it has provided for me," he explains.

At an age when most of us would say that society owes us and we've earned a rest, Jack is still finding ways to help. In doing so he shows that the struggle never ends, and neither does our capacity to triumph and our obligation to contribute to our community.

Linda Diebert, the executive director of the transit service, once said, "Jack is such a gentle hero. He has spent a lifetime using his special talents to get things done and to help others."

Says Jack: "I do what I can to be a good citizen."

ANN LIGUORI

When a Moment of Truth comes in the course of the daily battle to keep a career on track, it can be years before you recognize it for what it was. That seems to be especially true when you are young and life is a swift river that, from time to time, falls off into seething rapids full of rocks and eddies and undercurrents. At such times, all you want to do is ride it out, keep your head above water, not let it pull you under. And when you make it, relying only on your wits and strength, you're too busy being worried about the next stretch and the one after that to wonder whether that particular piece of angry water was the one that defined your journey. It was that way for Ann Liguori, when she was young and had a dream that she was determined to make happen. It was only when I talked to her for this book and asked her about a single meeting that she said, "Yes, that was my Moment of Truth."

Ann Liguori was not yet thirty, a fresh-faced young woman from Ohio as wholesome as a milk mustache. She had come to New York to follow a dream, and whether she made it or not would all come down to a single, defining moment.

She had formed the dream at the age of three when she saw a woman on television in her hometown of Cincinnati. The woman's name was Ruth Lyons, and she hosted a noon-hour talk show on WLW-TV, interviewing the most interesting and successful people in the city.

The little girl was mesmerized by the white-haired Lyons, captivated by her grace and elegance. "I knew right then that's what I was going to do," Liguori recalls.

She didn't know that the odds would be stacked against her; didn't know about the realities of the broadcast industry, where you can win a prestigious award one day and be out of work the next. Even years later, when she was learning her craft in college, she didn't understand what it would take.

That's one of the blessings of being young and taking on life for the first time. Sometimes the less you know, the better off you are. It is enough to believe in yourself and what you are doing so completely that the idea of failing never arises.

Even though Ann had formed her goal at a young age and never grown out of it, she lived her life fully in each moment. No matter what she did, whether it was school-work or sports, she had to be the best. Because she paid attention to details, she almost always was.

In high school, she was Ms. Everything. She won sixteen varsity letters in track, basketball, volleyball, and tennis. Because her school had no girls' tennis team, she went out for the boys' team and was the number one singles player. If that weren't enough, she was also homecoming queen.

Title IX, the federal law that demanded equal opportunities for women in high school and college athletics, was new in the late 1970s, and the scholarships for women athletes that are plentiful today had not yet materialized. So Ann's family paid her way to the University of South Florida in Tampa, where she majored in broadcast journalism.

Her college life mirrored her high school years, and success followed success. She worked at the campus radio station, interned for the local NBC affiliate TV station, produced and starred in a weekly show on cable television before anyone knew what cable was. "I tried to do everything," she says. For the most part, she did.

Reality struck during her junior year in 1981. First her father died of cancer. Nine months later her brother, one year older than she, died of leukemia.

The death of her brother—one of three siblings—came just as she was starting a prestigious fellowship in New York, which involved an internship at a major television station. She flew to Cleveland for her brother's funeral, and she considered staying with her family instead of returning to New York. "It was a tough decision. They only took twenty people in the whole country, and my whole future depended on this fellowship and being in New York," she recalls.

Ann was smart enough to realize that she could do more for her family by being what they wanted her to be—herself. At an early age, she had learned that life does—and must— go on, and the best way she could honor her brother was by refusing to quit. She decided to go back to New York.

Now she began to learn firsthand about big-city television. She quickly realized two things. First, she didn't want to take the long, vicious trek through the television-network career maze or work for someone else. Second, she wanted to stay involved with sports.

Again, she set herself apart from the crowd. Without thinking about the difficulties, she created a brief, recorded weekly radio commentary called "Ann Liguori, In the Line-Up," took it to sponsors, and sold it for broadcast throughout New England. That spot caught the attention of executives who were forming a new radio station in New York—WFAN—that would bring the novel concept of all-sports radio to the public. They didn't want Ann's recorded commentary. They wanted her—full-time and live.

It was the summer of 1987, and life was better than good. After several years of freelancing, she was a full-time reporter with her own weekly talk show on a pioneering station. Her first Saturday talk show was a coup—the first interview with Dwight Gooden, then the star pitcher for the New York Mets, after he had been discharged from a substance-abuse clinic.

"It was a dream job for anybody," she says. But, like a dream, it ended with a jolt. The new station had hired too many people in the heady days of its founding. Less than a year later, it pink-slipped twenty-five in one day, among them Ann. Suddenly she had rent payments to make, a life to support, and no income other than what she made from continuing her weekend talk show as a part-time job.

"I was devastated," she says. "It wasn't like we were fired because we weren't good. If you're an athlete and you win the race, you win the race. But in broadcasting, if you win the race, you can still get fired. It's brutal. You put your heart and soul into something. They tell you you're really good. You know you're really good. And you get the pink slip.

"At that point, you can either jump off the bridge or put your life together and move on."

But to what?

Ann did something else that is a mark of successful people. She didn't panic, and she didn't run out and take the first job she could find, just to have a paycheck. She fell back on her freelancing skills, writing for newspapers and magazines and getting quotes in locker rooms as a freelance radio reporter, eating the free buffets the local pro teams put out for the press, counting every dollar. And all the while, she was putting together a plan.

She wanted to start her own half-hour interview show on television. She had nothing with which to do it except her own confidence. That doesn't sound like much, but confidence in ourselves is the most powerful tool we have. And Ann needed every bit of hers. After all, no other woman hosted a sports interview program on television. For the testosterone-driven audience of New York, it was an idea as foreign as waiting for the light to change before crossing the street.

By all rights, she had no business even thinking she could succeed. A more sensible—or less determined—person would have realized the quest was hopeless and slunk back to Ohio, another kid chewed up by the New York meat grinder. Which only proves that being sensible isn't always the virtue it's purported to be.

"Everybody told me I was nuts. No way was I going to

get a show. Nobody had done what I was trying to do," she remembers. "There were many times when I thought, 'What am I doing here?' It was tough. I had no family in New York. I didn't have a support system."

Until then, she had not truly been tested in the dog-eat-dog world of business. Through her struggle, an experience that was new for someone who had always come out on top, Ann would gain empathy for the struggles of others, a valuable asset for an interviewer. It also taught her about living in the moment and tending to the details, because she never knew which moment would prove vital.

"I think my athletic training helped," she says of that difficult time and so many others that followed. "You learn how to win and lose. You develop discipline and self-esteem."

You learn to move on to the next point, the next game, the next season.

She pounded the streets between freelance gigs, trying to find a home for her show and the $130,000 it would take to produce the first thirteen shows. In 1989 she found a potential home. MSG Network, the cable station that carried the Knicks, Rangers, and Yankees had a half-hour slot they wanted to fill in the early evening. If they could do it without spending their own money, so much the better. Ann heard about it and offered to fill the slot.

They told her she was welcome to it. All she had to do was come up with the money to produce it. Again, her friends told her it was impossible. After all, this went beyond simply interviewing athletes. It involved selling advertising, putting together a production company, lining up guests, shooting the sessions, editing the tape, and doing the countless things that go into producing a sports interview show. MSG Network didn't even give her a studio. She would have to arrange for that as well.

"Nobody did all that," Ann says. "Certainly not someone in her mid-twenties who had no advertising experience."

She made appointments with advertising executives and began begging for dollars. "They would look at me, like, 'Who are you? And what do you want?' People work their whole lives to learn how to sell ads and package shows."

Liguori didn't have her whole life to learn. She had an opportunity now, and she would have to learn on the fly. Door after door closed in her face, until one idea popped into her head.

As a freelance reporter, she had covered a lot of professional tennis and had gotten to know a young man who did public relations for a company that ran a number of tennis tournaments under the sponsorship of Volvo. Ann asked her friend if he knew anyone who could help arrange a meeting with Volvo's American CEO. He did, and the meeting was arranged with the CEO and a Volvo marketing executive. The catch was that the marketing man didn't like the idea of sponsoring a woman doing a sports interview show, and Ann knew it. Her only hope was to get the CEO by himself. She didn't need long. Just a few minutes. But she couldn't have the marketing man undercutting her.

If her career had been a tennis match, Ann says now, "I was down 15–40 in the fifth game of the second set, having lost the first set. I was going to lose the match if I didn't get this guy to commit."

It would be her Moment of Truth, and all the success

that followed flowed from it. Not that she thought of it that way. At the time she was just doing what she had to do. The lasting change came from facing a make-or-break moment and coming up big, from fighting off break points and finally serving an ace and winning the match.

She played it like a tennis match, one point, one stroke at a time, refusing to accept the inevitability of defeat and going deep inside to discover a strategy that would work. She saw her opportunity in something as simple as a casual lunch. She suggested they pick up sandwiches. The CEO asked the marketing man to get them.

When the other man left, she quickly laid out her plans for the show and told the CEO what she needed to make it happen. "He loved the idea. By the time the other guy came back, the deal was done."

Thus was born *Sports Interview with Ann Liguori*, the longest-running television sports interview show hosted by a woman. From it came other shows, a book, and marriage to Steve Geller—the man she eventually hired to produce her show.

The television business gets more familiar, she says, but it never gets easier. Women are still a tiny minority in broadcast sports. Sponsors are fickle. Fame is fleeting. But for Ann Liguori it started with five minutes and a dream.

"I didn't appreciate those moments for what they were until years later," she says now. "The older you get, the more you know. I have agents calling me up now, asking, 'How do you do it?'

"It's still tough," she says. "Every day you're selling the show. Every day is a new Moment of Truth."

BERNARD MARCUS

If Bernard Marcus hadn't experienced his Moment of Truth, today he would be just another guy enjoying a well-earned retirement in Florida. But he got in the way of someone else's ambition, was thrown out of work, and watched everything he had struggled to build over twenty years melt away as he tried to right a wrong that couldn't be righted. Finally, faced with the prospect of fighting a war that would destroy him, he met a man who helped him to see that the way out lay in accepting the challenge of the future and not in living in the past. Because of that transforming moment, Bernie went on to change the way America shops.

He wanted to be a doctor, but there was no money for that dream, not for a kid who was born in 1929, the year of the Stock Market crash, and grew up, the son of Russian immigrants, in a tenement in Newark, New Jersey. So Bernard Marcus did the next best thing: He worked his way through Rutgers University and earned a pharmacist's degree.

But Bernie, as everyone knows him, wasn't meant to be a pharmacist either. He learned that when he took a job at Two Guys, a discount department store, and was put in charge of the cosmetics department. Bernie immersed himself in his work and found a home in discount marketing—a field on which he would put an indelible stamp.

For nearly twenty years, Bernie Marcus's trajectory through the business world was as steady and unerring as a career could be. He went from being an employee of Two Guys to president of O'Dell, a manufacturing company, where he learned what he already knew deep inside—that retailing was his real calling. Next he joined Vornado, a chain of discount stores, where he was vice president of hard goods merchandising. Finally he accepted the presidency of Handy Dan's, a discount hardware chain headquartered in California.

At Handy Dan's, Bernie joined forces with Arthur Blank, an accountant who became his best friend, confidant, right-hand man, and chief financial officer of the company. Together, they managed a thriving business. Each of their stores averaged $3 million in annual sales. Handy Dan's was a wholly owned subsidiary of the Daylin Corporation, a multifaceted firm that had fallen into bankruptcy. But Handy Dan's continued to thrive, and in one year provided a $7 million profit when the entire Daylin conglomerate earned only $7.8 million.

But as Bernie was soon to learn, being successful doesn't guarantee anything in life.

To haul itself out of bankruptcy, Daylin brought in the notorious Sanford C. "Sandy" Sigoloff as its CEO. Sigoloff already had a reputation as a man who did not get where he was by being easy to work for, a man who would rescue a company and, in the process, leave behind great mounds of broken careers. He reveled in the nickname Ming the Merciless, after the character in the old *Flash Gordon* serials.

Bernie didn't like Sigoloff, but he didn't really care if Sigoloff liked him. After all, Handy Dan's was making money and the company was a publicly traded entity answerable to stockholders. What could Sigoloff do? Fire him? Bernie thought that was impossible.

But Sigoloff couldn't stand the fact that Daylin's return from bankruptcy wasn't due entirely to his efforts, but owed its profit margin to Bernie's division. And as long as Bernie was there, Sigoloff couldn't take the credit for turning Daylin around.

As long as Handy Dan's was publicly traded, Sigoloff had a legal obligation to the shareholders to maintain fiscal responsibility. He couldn't fire a successful CEO. So Sigoloff bought out the outstanding Handy Dan's stock, removing Bernie's safety net. In short order, Sigoloff fired Bernie, Blank, and a number of other Handy Dan's executives, canceled their contracts, dared them to sue him, and, for good measure, accused Bernie before the Securities and Exchange Commission of engaging in unfair labor practices.

The year was 1978. Bernie Marcus was forty-nine years old and unemployed. Worst of all, his spotless reputation, built through nearly twenty years of hard work, was being dragged through the mud of the daily financial papers.

Bernie responded by doing what Americans often do in such situations. He sued.

Our litigious society teaches us that this is what we are supposed to do. But it doesn't teach us about the costs of pursuing our enemies through the courts. As Bernie would learn, the price is taken not only out of our wallets but also out of our souls.

Bernie told me, "My attorney said, 'You have a great case. We can win.' But every time I talked to him, it cost me two hundred dollars an hour."

Bernie was married and had three kids. Because of the charges Sigoloff brought against him—none of which were ever found to have any basis in fact—nobody wanted to hire him. His money was running out. For the first time in his life, he found that he couldn't sleep at night, and he was consumed by self-doubt.

"I had never faced anything like that before in my whole life," Bernie says. "The whole thing was unreal. It was unjust. I imagined what it must be like for someone who is accused of committing a crime when he was at home in bed.

"This was so wrong, so illogical. How do you deal with something like that? It didn't make any sense to me.

"When something unjust happens to you," he continues, "you question your own sanity, your own ability. You ask yourself, 'What could I have done?' You keep looking back rather than looking forward. It begins to preoccupy your mind completely."

He became fixated on getting revenge, on winning his

lawsuit. The problem was that Sigoloff was playing this game with Daylin's money, while Bernie was playing with his own. It was a game that, even if he won, Bernie would lose.

He was so close to the situation, though, that he couldn't see the truth of it. In Greek drama, when things have come to such a pass, and it seems as if no earthly power can save the hero, the dramatist falls back on a device called deus ex machina—literally, the "god from the machine." The machine was a crane that lowered a god from the sky to solve the problem.

Bernie's deus ex machina was Sol Price, the founder of the Price Club discount shopping chain. He and Bernie had known each other for some time, and one day Sol, knowing about Bernie's troubles, invited Bernie to his home in San Diego.

Sol was having legal problems of his own with a German outfit that had bought out one of his companies. The Germans had broken their contract with Sol, and Sol had initiated legal proceedings against them three years earlier.

When Bernie arrived at Sol's home, Sol took him to a spare bedroom, opened the door, and invited Bernie to have a look. What Bernie saw astonished him. The entire room, from floor to ceiling, was filled with stacks of legal folders.

"This is what I have spent the last three years of my life going through," Sol said. It wasn't something he did just when he had the time. Every minute of his life, every day, was consumed by the lawsuit. "The attorneys are sucking me dry," Sol said. "In the final analysis, even if I win, I lose."

At that moment, Bernie saw not Sol's present but his own future. And he realized this wasn't what he wanted for his life.

This, says Bernie, was his Moment of Truth. "Sol essentially slapped me in the face," he says.

If this was justice, was it worth it? And even if he won, what would it get him? Money could not wipe away the bitterness that such a battle could only nurture. He had spent his life creating new ways of doing things, and now he was interested only in destroying. Until that moment, he hadn't realized that he wasn't destroying Sig Sigoloff. He was destroying himself.

Sol fired a series of questions at Bernie. "Do you think you're creative? Can you be successful? Are you good at what you do?"

Wallowing in self-pity and hurt, Bernie hadn't even thought of those things—the things that had carried him through what had been a brilliant career. "For the first time," he says, "I looked at myself realistically. Yes, I am creative. Yes, I'm good at what I do. Yes, I can be successful.

"I will be successful."

With his own future arrayed so nightmarishly in Sol Price's spare room, Bernie realized this wasn't the way to get even with Sigoloff. "Sol said, 'The best way to win is to become successful. Trust me.' "

Sol told Bernie to call Sigoloff, tell him where to go and what to do with his suit, pay off the lawyers, and get back to creating, to doing.

"It was time to get on with my life," says Bernie.

The key word is "life." What he was doing wasn't anything like the life he had known. That life was full of improving the way things were done. It was exciting and energizing, fulfilling and rewarding. The world of lawyers he had entered had none of those qualities. Sol really was right, and not just for Bernie. He was right for all of us. There is more than one way to get even, and the best way is to succeed in spite of everything.

"That's the way I won," he says. "I won in the real world."

He stopped worrying about Sigoloff and started thinking about an idea he had all but forgotten. It was a new concept in hardware and building supplies that would come to be called the Home Depot. For years, Bernie had dreamed of building a superstore with 100,000 square feet of space—three times the size of a Handy Dan's—and offering 40,000 to 50,000 separate items. Instead of running on a margin of better than 40 percent, he would sell at margins of under 30 percent and make up the difference in volume. His employees would be partners in the company, and they would be highly trained to instruct do-it-yourselfers on how to complete a project. He—together with Arthur Blank—would make Handy Dan's obsolete.

Getting the financing wasn't easy, but with the assistance of Ken Langone, a New York investment banker, Bernie and Blank got it done.

The rest, as they say, is history. By the year 2000, Home Depots were ubiquitous across the landscape in the United States and Canada. The deals that Bernie and Arthur offered were so good that even contractors bought their supplies there.

And it all happened because that was where the struggle led a man with an idea.

Bernie retired from the day-to-day running of the

company in 1997, but remained as chairman of the board while Arthur Blank became chief executive officer. Closing in on seventy years of age, Bernie turned his attention to giving away the nearly $2 billion he had earned from his company.

He made one donation of $45 million to the Kennedy Krieger Institute, a Baltimore-based organization dedicated to treating children with developmental disabilities of all kinds. Bernie and his wife, Billi, decided to make the gift to establish a national network of facilities for such children after they saw a Home Depot employee struggle to find services for his retarded child.

Bernie has established the Marcus Foundation and the Marcus Center, two other charitable enterprises that target children in need. In 1999 he was voted the Most Respected CEO in Atlanta, his company's headquarters, by readers of the *Atlanta Business Chronicle*, and he was named Philanthropist of the Year by the National Society of Fundraising Executives. He is also a member of the National Entrepreneurs' Hall of Fame.

All in all, it's been a lot more satisfying than suing Sandy Sigoloff.

"What I've learned is not to look back," Bernie says now. "The only time I look back is to learn a lesson. I'm living today. I'm concerned with tomorrow and the day after. If you totally focus on yesterday, you lose tomorrow. That's what happened to me when I got fired from Handy Dan's.

"If you're negative, the whole world is negative. If every time you try you think you're going to fail, you fail. If you think positively, you're ahead. If you're a whiner, you can't be a winner."

JULIA STEWART

If you are sick, you go to a doctor. But if your family is sick, and you're just a kid, where do you go? This is the question Julia Stewart faced when she was twelve years old. It is easy to stand back and say she could have gone to her principal or clergyman or a social service agency, but what would any of us have done in such a situation nearly thirty years ago? If she tried to explain that her parents were making her life a living hell, who would have believed her? Even if someone did, what could they do? She wasn't being abused by any legal definition of that word, but her parents' hatred for each other was making her miserable. The action Julia took was born out of the absolute necessity of doing something. Sometimes that's all that's required—taking action when no one else will.

Fifteen or twenty years ago, when I was still working in Dallas, I met Julia Stewart. She was a young, up-and-coming food service executive, full of ambition and life. I was a member of the board of directors for Tony Roma's at the time and was asked to interview her for an executive position.

We met for dinner, and to be honest, I don't remember much about the interview other than that she decided not to take the offer. Our business discussion lasted only about fifteen minutes, but dinner lasted six hours. When it was over, I had lost a potential top executive for Tony Roma's, but I had gained a friend for life.

When I met her, Julia had just started a remarkable career that has since broken ground in many different ways. She told me she grew up in the fifties and sixties as an only child, the daughter of two high school educators in the San Diego area. She was student body president of her high school, anchored the champion 440 relay for the track team, and led the speech club. She got a scholarship to the speech team at the University of California–Santa Barbara, and enrolled in the premed program.

"I was a pathology-audiology major," she says. "I was going to teach the world to speak. I wanted to help people better themselves."

One of her professors saw in her the potential to pursue a very different career. "He said that the medical profession is mostly in black and white and that I saw a lot of gray areas. He told me he thought I would be miserable because I had a lot of creative energy. He suggested I talk to a professor in the marketing and communication school, where I could put my creativity to better use."

The professor was right, and Julia transferred out of pre-med. It was one of the few times in her life when she needed a little bit of help to see where she was going. Even then, she was a force of nature, as relentless as the surf, as constant and dependable as the trade winds. Nothing stops her. Nothing slows her down. And like the wind and the surf, she is untutored. Her drive to be the best, to treat obstacles as if they aren't there, is as fundamental to her as hydrogen and oxygen are to water.

"People ask me who my mentor was, and they get offended when I tell them I didn't have one," she says. "But it's the truth. I don't ever remember anyone showing me the way."

Certainly not after she changed majors. After graduating, she landed a job for a company in San Diego running its in-house ad agency. It was a good first job, but Julia found it wasn't exactly what she wanted. "In that position I recommended and others decided," she says. "I wanted to run things, to be the one who acted on the recommendations of others."

She knew intuitively that just because a job is comfortable doesn't mean it's right. What she needed now was something to spark her interest. It wasn't long in coming.

One day, she had to fly to a meeting in New York. As she was reading the *Wall Street Journal* on the plane, the man sitting next to her—a big, burly fellow with a personality to match his frame—said, "It looks like you're looking for a job."

"Nah," she said. "I like reading the *Journal*."

The man introduced himself as Carl Karcher. She would learn later that Karcher was the founder of Carl's Jr. Restaurants and a brilliant businessman. He kept talking to her, sounding out her ideas and her goals.

Finally, he said, "I like you. You're full of spunk. You're the kind of person I'm looking for. You have to come and work for me."

There was no turning him down. From then on, Julia was launched on a career that by 1998 would make her the first woman chief operating officer of a major food service company—Applebee's Restaurants, the largest casual-dining chain in the world.

I had anticipated that Julia would consider the chance meeting with Karcher to be her Moment of Truth. Either that or later in her career, when she was working for Burger King and accepted an offer at Taco Bell, where she broke gender barriers by moving from marketing to actually running the show.

When I contacted Julia to do this book, I learned that as well as I thought I knew Julia, there was a lot about her I didn't know—that, in fact, almost nobody knew. Her Moment of Truth had taken place many years before, when she was twelve years old and living with two parents who despised each other. It was a part of her life she hadn't told me about before.

Her father was a high school history teacher and her mother was a physical education teacher. He was brilliant. "One of the most brilliant men I've ever known," she says. "My father could have solved world hunger if he had decided to. But he was a dreamer, and he was self-destructive. He never did the things he could have."

It was apparent early in the marriage, which was necessitated by the fact that his wife-to-be was pregnant with Julia, that the pair were a complete mismatch. "My mother was the daughter of illiterate parents who didn't speak English," Julia says. "She had a head for money and figures. She was a doer. Both of my parents were remarkable in their own ways." And together, they were remarkably miserable.

"It was probably inevitable that they would get divorced," she says now. Whatever hurt her parents' feuding caused has long since been expunged. She remembers them screaming constantly at each other, calling each other vile names. Each parent put the other in the hospital. It was a miracle that neither killed the other.

Perhaps Julia's good fortune—if you could find good fortune in such circumstances—was that her parents didn't take out their anger on her, as is so common in bad marriages. Both loved her as well as they could, approved of her constantly, never belittled or demeaned her.

Still, the tension between the two was more than any child should have to bear. Julia knew they should be divorced and suspected they were staying together for her sake. So, at the age of twelve, she did the only thing she could think of to force a change. She ran away from home.

That was her real Moment of Truth, the moment when she decided that there must be a way to take control of her life, when she decided that if she didn't do something her parents would never see what they were doing to themselves and to her.

"I got together with a friend whose home life was much worse than mine. We got on a bus and went north," she says, not finding what she did all that remarkable. "We came back after two days."

When she got back, she told her parents why she had left. "Is it that bad?" her father asked her. Yes, she said, it was that bad and worse.

"That was the first time I ever saw my father cry," she says. Within the next day or two, he moved out and the couple got a divorce.

"By getting on that bus I said, 'I want more,' " Julia says. "I was so well beyond my years. I was twelve going on thirty."

Ever since she was little, Julia had always wanted to help people make things right. She was always organizing kids on her street or in school, trying to make life better for all of them. Maybe that's what you do when the one place you can't do anything about is your own home.

"I knew something wasn't right at home," she says. "I knew other people didn't live like we did. I remember lying about my home life, because I didn't want people to know. I just didn't understand. I didn't want to be like my parents. I didn't want to be self-destructive.

"My mother had been raised on a farm. She was trying to rise above her past. But she was raised in an environment where they didn't touch, didn't show affection or love. I knew there was a bigger, brighter world, and I was going to go get it."

After the divorce, Julia tried living first with her mother, then with her father, then back with her mother. Neither situation was good for her, and she realized that if she wanted some form of a normal life, she would have to create it for herself. And that would require money. So, at the age of fourteen, she got a job as a telephone solicitor.

"I was working illegally," she admits. "I couldn't go to the office to pick up my paycheck for fear they'd find out how young I was. I asked them to mail the check to my home."

"I always wanted to earn my own living," she says. "Money meant independence."

Two years later, when she was sixteen and a junior in high school, she took the next step—she moved out of her mother's home. With her mother's approval—"What was she going to say? It was obvious I could take care of myself"—she rented a furnished one-bedroom apartment for a hundred dollars a month, got a job busing tables in a restaurant, bought a car, and took care of herself.

"I got four hours' sleep each night," she says. "I've always been lucky in that I don't need a lot of sleep. And I was always going to make my life better. I was earning a living. I was student body president, was on the track team, the speech team, the drama team."

Making her own decisions, picking her own friends, coming to her own moral judgments, Julia found her path. "I could have gone a lot of different ways," she admits. "I tried hanging out with all the groups in high school—the druggies, the socialites, the athletes, the student government types."

But she had enough sense of who she was, and what she

wanted, to know that none of the superficial lifestyles typical of high school cliques were meant for her.

"I wanted more than that," she says of the artificial ca-
maraderie of high school. "I never really hung with anyone.
I took a great deal of pride in the fact that no one could cate-
gorize me. I was a different animal."

I knew none of this about her. No one did. In dozens of
interviews with magazines and newspapers, no one had
ever tried to find out who she really was. So she kept it to
herself. Besides, it was all water over the dam, and Julia has
never lived in the past. She has always lived beyond today,
somewhere in a future that only she sees.

"People assume I was born with a silver spoon in my
mouth," she says today of those who meet the polished, articulate, decisive executive who is Julia Stewart. "People
make incredible assumptions about my personal life, none
of which are true. I just have incredibly well-adjusted self-
esteem. I feel good about myself. I'm proud of myself."

Ask her where that comes from, and she pauses, then
says quietly, "I don't know."

Maybe she simply won the genetic sweepstakes, getting
all the best qualities of her parents and none of the worst.
It's as good an explanation as any.

Change comes only through hard work. Julia's spec-
tacular rise through the corporate ranks came at the price
of a lot of self-sacrifice. For years, she had the most meager
kind of social life.

But she wouldn't settle for anything less than the best in
a husband, either. She finally met Jon Greenawalt while she
was working for Burger King and headquartered in San

Francisco. She moved to Taco Bell, and loved her new life as a married woman and her business life as the chief executive of a vast territory that generated $2 billion in annual sales. When she gave birth to a son, Alec, the perfect life she had longed for as a child seemed to be complete.

Julia thought she would stay with Taco Bell for the rest of her career. But in 1998 she got a call. Applebee's Restaurants wanted to hire her as its president. The position offered everything she wanted. With 1,200 restaurants, Applebee's is the largest chain of its kind in the world. She would have total control of the entire company and would be one of the few women in such a position, a true trailblazer.

The job meant a move to Kansas City, Kansas. Jon, himself a successful executive, quit his job and formed a new business in Kansas in order to be with her. Julia dove into her work. But she soon noticed that she wasn't feeling well in the mornings, and her period stopped. A trip to the doctor confirmed that she was pregnant with her second child.

"Can you imagine?" she says. She was in her late forties, and she had thought that another pregnancy was out of the question. She had thought wrong.

"Three months after I started work, I had to tell Applebee's that I was pregnant," she says. "They said, 'This is a joke, right?'" She told them it wasn't, but don't worry, everything would be fine.

You hear stories about pioneer women working in the fields and stopping to deliver a baby. Well, Julia was the modern equivalent. She entered the labor room with her cell phone and conducted business and conference calls as she was in labor. As soon as her daughter, Aubrey, was born, she was back on the phone, back to work. She was right. Everything was fine.

That was in the early summer of 1999, and the addition of Aubrey to the family made her world complete. She cherishes her family. "Every day I tell my children I love them," she says. "Every day." Then she adds, "I'm a very lucky woman."

She has made peace with her parents, accepted them for who they are. She does a lot of charity work and sits on boards of major organizations, including the Women's Food Service Forum, which she and eleven other women formed a number of years ago to support career advancement for women in the industry.

Although retirement is a long way away, she already knows what she will do when she steps down from Applebee's. "When I retire from this rat race," she says, with her trademark certainty, "I absolutely will go back to college, get my credentials, and teach."

That was her original goal—to help children learn to speak. She fell into the food service business, and she loves her work. But in the back of her mind she still wants to be a simple teacher. It will be her way of helping other kids from troubled homes to do the things she has done, to pass on what she has learned. And it will be a testament to her parents.

"The best thing about my parents," she says, "was that over the course of their careers, they touched people's lives. To listen to people who had them in school talk about my parents and what great teachers they were brings tears to my eyes. They always wanted to teach kids to make the world a better place."

Even though her parents weren't always there for her, Julia says, "I never felt unloved. There are a lot of people whose lives were a lot worse than mine. I never forget where I came from."

She feels certain that someday, when people talk about Julia Stewart, what they will remember most "won't be that I was president of Applebee's. It will be that I made the world a richer, better place for a lot of people. I want that to be my legacy."

STEPHEN AND ELIZABETH WAMPLER

A common thread that I find in people who were guided by necessity to their Moment of Truth is that they didn't let others tell them what they could or couldn't do. Each one of them had an idea and went with it, not because someone else said it was right but because he or she decided it was right. Stephen and Elizabeth Wampler exemplify this concept perfectly. What makes their Moment so special is that they faced it at the beginning of their life together, and in doing so they became partners not just in life but in business as well.

Stephen Wampler has always had a wide streak of independence.

Exercising that independence wasn't easy for him growing up. He was born with cerebral palsy in suburban San Francisco and has been confined all his life to a motorized wheelchair. He never saw his disability as a hindrance, something that I find is common among people who are born with debilitating conditions. When you grow up with something, it is normal to you. Only to others does it seem a trial.

He grew up cheerful and extroverted, thinking there wasn't much he couldn't do. But he wanted to be his own man, leave the security of home and parents, be in control of his own life. So, despite his parents' objections, Stephen went to the University of California–Davis at the opposite end of the state, where he took up engineering.

"Davis is like a Midwest town," Stephen says. "I could get to everything by myself. Where we lived in the Bay Area was on top of a hill. It was in the middle of nowhere, and I couldn't get anywhere by myself."

He led a normal college life, going to parties, dating, being on his own. When he graduated, he slid right into a job as an environmental engineer at RayChem, a company in San Diego. He set up housekeeping on Coronado Island, a mile-square community that was compact enough to bring all the necessities of life within convenient wheelchair distance.

The only thing Stephen really needed help with was getting to and from work, because he couldn't drive a car. He hired a woman in his neighborhood to be his driver, and one day when she arrived to pick him up at work she had another woman with her.

Her name was Elizabeth, and she had just moved to Coronado Island, even though, as she says, "I really couldn't afford to live there." A native of the San Diego area, she was closing in on her thirtieth birthday but really just beginning her life.

She had gone to college, but when she should have been starting on a career, her father took ill. "He was a colonel in the Marine Corps," she says. When she was growing up, the oldest of three children, she remembers her father as every inch a marine. "He was healthy and fit. He ran every day and worked out," she says. "Then he got a brain tumor."

He went from being a man who could do anything to one who needed constant care. Elizabeth moved in across the street from her parents and took on the job of being her father's attendant. He fought the disease for seven years before it took his life, and she nursed him the entire time.

Although Elizabeth didn't know it then, what she thought of as a tragedy would eventually become a blessing. She learned how to care for another person. When the time came, that knowledge opened her up to a love she otherwise would not have found.

She has no regrets about the years she lost. "I wouldn't have traded the experience of taking care of my father for anything," she says. "After he died, I moved to Coronado as a treat for myself. It's a very beautiful place, and I was able to afford it by moving in with the woman who was Stephen's driver."

Elizabeth had half heard Stephen's story and had mentally changed cerebral palsy—a condition she had never heard of—into cystic fibrosis. She didn't know much about that either, except that it was eventually fatal. Or so she thought.

So, she says, when she first saw Stephen coming out of work in his chair, "the first thing I thought was, 'He's so handsome.' My second thought was, 'I don't want to cry in front of him,' because I thought he had cystic fibrosis and was going to die."

Stephen was blissfully ignorant of Elizabeth's emotional struggle. He was preoccupied with other things, he says, and "I really didn't notice her. I didn't pay any attention to her that first day at all."

But they kept running into each other in the small community of Coronado and became casual friends. Then one night, about a month after she moved in, Elizabeth's roommate had a dinner party and invited Stephen. During dinner, Elizabeth sat across from him. "I noticed we both laughed at the same things and that we had a lot in common."

Elizabeth realized she had met the man with whom she wanted to spend her life. "I fell in love with him instantly," she says, her voice effervescent. "It was pretty overpowering. My attraction came out of nowhere. I had never known anyone in a wheelchair."

She says that taking care of her father during his long illness made her receptive to the idea of marrying someone who had a disability. "I would not be with Stephen if I hadn't gone through what I did with my dad. I wondered if it would be difficult," she admits, "but I didn't care. By the time we had our first date, I could have married him the next day."

They dated for a long time, and Elizabeth found that being with Stephen presented no problems at all. "It's the exact opposite," she says. "It's like living with a celebrity. Everyone in Coronado knows Stephen."

Elizabeth got a job with a hotel, and the couple set a wedding date well in advance. They were both working and earning good money. They bought a house and started planning for a big wedding—350 people with all the trimmings.

Life was wonderful and was only going to get better. Then, in 1995, six weeks before the wedding, Stephen came home from work and told Elizabeth that his company had been bought out and the facility he worked in was going to be shut down. He would continue working for a while, but for all intents and purposes he was without a job.

They knew he would have trouble finding another job because of his disability. "People don't want to hire somebody who's disabled," he says without a shred of bitterness.

It wasn't personal. They both knew that. "It's just a natural prejudice people have," she says, her voice matter-of-fact. Stephen, who shares her utter lack of ill will toward anyone or anything, agrees.

At least Elizabeth had her job to carry them along while Stephen looked for work, and she was doing fabulously in it. "I had been working at my job for three years. Getting promoted regularly. A raise every six months. I thought everything was going great."

A week and a half went by. Steve picked up the phone at work and heard Elizabeth's voice.

"Honey," she began, "you're not going to believe this, but I'm sitting at home."

"Why?" he responded. "Is the car broken down?"

"No," she replied. "We all got let go today. The hotel was sold."

The wedding was three weeks away.

"That," they say together, "was our Moment of Truth." They decided that somehow, some way, they were going to make it. They believed in each other, and that was enough.

Others in different circumstances might have canceled expensive plans. But Stephen and Elizabeth believed that the wedding was their statement to the world of their commitment, and even though it would cost thousands of dollars they could have put toward food and housing, they refused to scale it back.

"It was an enormous affair," Elizabeth says. "People came from all over the country." On what is normally one of the happiest days of a couple's lives, Stephen and Elizabeth knew that when the wedding was over, waiting for them would be a big mortgage and no money to pay it.

They had to cancel the honeymoon trip. That saved some money, but they still needed to find work.

They weren't naive about their situation. They were both old enough to know that their path was uncertain. But they also weren't going to settle for just anything. Even though they didn't know exactly where they were going, they were determined that when they got there, it would have been worth the effort.

One day, while they were trying to figure out what to do, they went down to the Coronado Hotel, a beautiful facility with large outdoor public spaces. They sat at a table to be alone and talk seriously about their future, tossing ideas back and forth.

"We were really giving ourselves a pep talk," says Elizabeth. "You know, 'Everything's going to be fine.' We didn't really believe it, but we were saying it."

As they were talking, an eccentric old man approached their table. He was wearing polyester from head to toe—shorts, shirt, and jacket—with a plastic visor on his head and black wing-tipped shoes. "His clothes were filthy," Elizabeth adds.

Almost anyone else would have chased the old man away, but Stephen and Elizabeth aren't that kind of people. Although they tried to ignore him, he started talking to them and wouldn't stop.

"He hadn't heard anything we'd been saying to each other," Elizabeth says, her voice filled with wonder. "He didn't know we didn't have jobs, or that we didn't know what to do with ourselves. He walked over and said, 'Here's what you have to do. This is the idea that you're looking for.' "

With that, the man, whose name they would later learn was Robert Sammon, began telling them about a business that he had wanted to start for fifty years. He had been a sailor, and then he became a drunk, and now he had no one—no family, no friends. He was eighty-five years old and suffering from alcoholic psychosis, so at times he went off on tangents that made no sense.

But he kept coming back to his idea, and when he did, his thoughts and speech became as clear as a bell. The idea was that there ought to be a business that arranges conventions for companies, a sort of travel agent/ombudsman. Travel agents work with individuals or tour groups, he said, but this would be for a business or group that wanted, say, five hundred hotel rooms in Richmond, Virginia, and also needed catering, transportation, flowers, and any number of other services.

A company would call this business, and it would contact every hotel in the Richmond area with that many rooms, work out packages, and present the packages to the client. When the client chose one, Stephen and Elizabeth would make the reservations and get a commission. They would take care of all the other arrangements the same way.

They would make their money not from the client but, like a travel agent, by taking a commission from the suppliers.

Sammon wouldn't stop talking. There's no telling how many others he had belabored with his idea over the years, but however many it was, they all doubtless felt the same way Stephen and Elizabeth did—the idea was too obvious. There must be thousands of companies that already provided such services. When was this strange old bird going to give up and leave?

After some twenty minutes, the old man tottered away, and Elizabeth and Stephen went back to their own discussion. They went home and didn't really think about it. Finally, tired and anxious about the future, they went to bed.

At three in the morning, both of them woke up together, looked at each other, and said, "Let's do it."

This story contains a huge lesson. One of the flaws in my character which I fight all the time is impatience. If someone had come up to me and rambled on as Sammon did to the Wamplers, I probably wouldn't have listened. But the Wamplers were not only polite enough to let him talk and patient enough to sit through his speech, they also listened. And you never know where you will find the missing piece of a puzzle. Especially when times are difficult, you have to be most open to the world and all its possibilities.

The next morning they got up and went to the library and found that Sammon was right. No business such as he described existed.

Once they were certain that they had come upon an unfilled need, they started planning how to go about setting up their business. They told their parents what they intended to do, and their parents told them they were crazy. What they should both have done was get new jobs and get on with their lives.

The couple didn't listen. Instead, they threw themselves into what was now more than a business. It was a dream.

"We maxed out our credit cards," says Elizabeth. "It was incredibly difficult financially for the first year and a half. It's a miracle we were able to pay the mortgage."

"We were looking for money in the couch cushions," adds Stephen.

"While we were starving," Elizabeth picks up, "we had to learn how to run a company, get clients, handle all the interoffice paperwork, figure out what forms we needed. It was terrifying. Our parents fought us all the way, but we just knew it would happen."

They had two friends who were self-made multimillionaires, and they kept going back to them for advice. "We asked them to play devil's advocate," Elizabeth says. "We wanted them to be as hard on us as they could be. They were incredibly helpful."

But while the friends were being helpful, they were also less than sanguine about the chances of the new business. "They told us later that three or four months after we started, they were talking about the odds of our making it. They gave us a ten percent chance," Elizabeth says. The friends kept that to themselves, telling the Wamplers only after their business took off.

It wasn't all bad. In a way, they both say, the year and a half it took to start showing a profit was the happiest time of their lives.

They got up at seven every morning and kept working until three in the morning.

"It was like a rite of passage," says Stephen. "We were very, very, very creative."

"Every decision was ours," Elizabeth adds. "It was a blast. We put ourselves in the minds of our future clients. If we were sitting in their shoes, how would we do that? That's what we got to do for a year. And we were doing it together. It turned out to be a pretty good honeymoon."

At last everything was in place, including the company's name—The Convention Company. All they needed to do was start calling potential clients and make a sale. The way Elizabeth saw it, you may as well have said all she needed to do was climb Mount Everest naked.

Despite all her talent and natural good spirits, Elizabeth was terrified of calling someone cold and trying to sell them something they had never heard of. But there was no alternative. Because of his cerebral palsy, Stephen does not talk clearly. He was the organizational force, the partner who would keep the books, the schedules, and see to all the other details of running the business. She had to do the selling.

She put it off and put it off. Finally, Stephen said to her as he left to run errands one day, "Promise me you'll make one call today."

Elizabeth promised. She made one call, and then another. On the second call, she made their first sale.

She had discovered out of necessity what born salespeople know by instinct. You can't make a sale without making contact. And every person who says no is one closer to the person who will say yes. What's more, Elizabeth also learned that she could do things she never dreamed of—if only she put her mind to it.

The business turned out to be everything Robert Sammon had said it would be. As sales climbed, the Wamplers, who still work out of an office in their house, took on help and watched the sea of debt in which they had become immersed turn into profit.

By 1998, they decided they were firmly enough established to start the family they had always wanted. Their daughter was born healthy and perfect. One day, when she was exactly six weeks old, Elizabeth was especially struck by the many blessings in her life.

"I was working and the baby was sleeping in the swing we bought for her," she says. "I suddenly realized that if I had gone back to work, this would be the day that my maternity leave would have been over, and I would have been gone. I just started crying."

"This is one of the greatest jobs I could ever think of doing," says Stephen. "We get to sit at home, work, have fun with really good clients. We have great staff. We don't have to deal with driving to work. We can come and go as we want."

They know just how lucky they are, and how what could have been a tragedy turned into the best break of their lives.

"We wouldn't have done it if we'd had jobs," Elizabeth says. "We wouldn't have had the nerve to quit. The best thing that ever happened to us was losing our jobs."

PART THREE

Moments of Truth Lie in Discovering Who You Really Are

*S*ome people find that their Moment of Truth arrives in an instant and utterly transforms their lives. They realize that the life they were living is not the life they were meant to live. For the first time they see clearly who they really are and what they are really meant to do.

Often they knew that an important part of life was missing for them, but they didn't know what it was. Sometimes the rebirth they experience is the result of a long process of self-discovery, made more difficult by their unfocused search for something they could not name. When they finally make their discovery, it's like uncovering a buried treasure chest, throwing up the lid, and being dazzled by the light reflected off the riches inside.

Nile Rodgers is one of the late twentieth century's great popular music innovators. For him, the night fell so slowly during years of substance abuse that it was years before he *realized he could no longer see. When his Moment of Truth came, it was immediate and absolute.*

For Bill Parcells the awakening came during a year of self-imposed exile from the game he loved. He discovered that he had given up more than a job coaching football. He had given up the one thing that made him truly alive.

The Moment of Truth for NBA basketball star Jayson Williams arrived in a moment of immature recklessness. It opened his eyes to the anger he had been carrying in his heart over the death of two of his sisters, years earlier.

Finally, Chris Evans, the owner of a limousine service in Dallas, found his Moment of Truth when he realized how disappointed his father was in him. His is a story of the transforming power of love.

NILE RODGERS

The road to rock-and-roll immortality is littered with dead bodies. Jim Morrison, Mama Cass, Jerry Garcia, Jimi Hendrix, Kurt Cobain—the list goes on. It is the dark side of sex, drugs, and rock and roll, the side we are never fully aware of until the coroner is called in. Nile Rodgers can tell you how innocently it starts. There are kids and there is music and there is freedom and there are parties. At first, it is wild and wonderful. You are young and bulletproof and will live forever. The drugs make you high and the sex makes you happy and the crowds and the money they spend to hear the music makes it a dream. It's hard, maybe impossible, to tell someone just starting in the business that the dream eventually becomes a nightmare and that the wild life can become living death—if you are fortunate enough not to die outright. Nile Rodgers lived it, saw his spirit die in it, and was finally reborn. He is one of the lucky ones.

Nile Rodgers fell for the guitar almost by accident, and he fell hard. He was born with music inside him and the guitar let it out. Together, they made sounds no one had made before.

Music took him around the world, earned him scads of money, and made him one of the most prolific and influential producers and musicians in modern history. He was the first to record a song with the subsonic bass line that has become the signature of modern pop music. As a studio musician, he has backed up everyone from Michael Jackson to Madonna. He has produced dozens of albums by a wide range of artists. Among those he has significantly influenced are Diana Ross, Sister Sledge, the Sugar Hill Gang, David Bowie, Mick Jagger, Cyndi Lauper, Al Jarreau, Duran Duran, Madonna, Queen—and that's not even half the list.

But the music also introduced him to a demon called drugs—bottles, cans, pills, joints, snorts, tabs. At first, alcohol and drugs were his friends. They let him perform, braced him to face tens of thousands of screaming fans.

Nile had been playing the guitar for nearly ten years beginning in the late 1960s, performing first on *Sesame Street*, joining or forming one band after another, experimenting with all the sounds that could be plucked and strummed and wrenched and pounded and tweaked and tickled out of a vibrating string of steel or gut. Finally, with a band called Chic, he created a new sound built on a primal bass beat, and a song called "Dance, Dance, Dance." Suddenly he was a star.

One night he was playing in a club in Atlantic City. The next night, he was standing offstage, gaping awestruck and terrified at 75,000 people in California's Oakland Coliseum, wondering how, in just a few minutes, he could walk out there and not faint.

"I had never seen anything like that," he says, looking back across the years to 1977. "I was so nervous I was shaking."

One of the roadies—the people who travel with a band and do all the grunt work that needs to be done for a little bit of money and a lot of reflected glory—handed Nile a big Styrofoam cup filled with beer. He poured it down his throat in one great draught, the foam biting his throat, the alcohol swarming into his bloodstream. He tossed the cup aside and screamed, "OAKLAND!"

Just like that, the terror was tamed. He found the roadie after Chic had driven the crowd wild and gave him an order. "Be sure you get me one of those before every concert."

Nile says of the alcohol, "It started to tell me it was my ally, and it was." It wasn't as if he was an alcoholic. It was just there to help him. "All my life, I was painfully shy," he says. "So much so that I would perform with my back to the audience. I was just afraid of people. And alcohol taught me how to be a performer, how to overcome that shyness. It was courage in a bottle.

"I thought I could take it or leave it," he says now, going on seven years since he finally faced the truth about his ally. "Little did I know."

You can hear those same words in any city or town in any of the thousands of Alcoholics Anonymous meetings held every day of the week, every hour of the day. The world of pop music may be a special world, but the world of addiction is not.

Nile had been around drugs and alcohol for what seemed all his life. He was conceived on Christmas 1951, the night his mother, a girl thirteen years of age, gave her virginity to his father. She was fourteen when he was born, and emotionally unequipped to be a mother. So Nile was raised by an ever-changing cast of grandparents, aunts, and sometimes, when she was in the mood, even his mother.

As a kid, he sifted the seeds out of the leaves of pot stashes. And as he grew, he tried everything that everyone else was doing in those days. "I sniffed glue, smoked banana peels, did it all," he says. He doesn't even remember when he first did drugs. "They were always around," he says. "It wasn't an event."

It wasn't the best childhood. "When I take the rose-colored spectacles off, it was weird," he says. And he remembers always trying to find ways to impress his mother, to get a little bit of attention.

"My earliest memories are of trying to please her," he says. "I'd try to do clever things—'Hey! Look at me! Look what I did!' Then I went into a fantasy life, a real Walter Mitty thing."

At an early age he found himself being sent to psychiatrists. But he says, "I wasn't nuts. I just wanted a mother. I was looking for approval."

He was a bright student and the only black kid in his

school. In those days students were held back if they failed, not blithely shipped on to the next grade. And Nile Rodgers knew that no matter what else happened to him, he wasn't going to be held back.

He sees two Moments of Truth in his life. The first came when he was fourteen. His mother decided to move to California. Nile was determined to stay in New York. He ran away from home, found friends to stay with, set his course on the future.

"I realized I had to make it in the world by myself," he says. "It was terrifying, but the fear of doing it the other way—of leaving New York—was greater. My mom went to California and I stayed behind. I was self-sufficient in mind and deed."

Without a real family, he looked for support groups all over the city. He drew joy from helping others, so he volunteered at the Salvation Army, hung out at coffee shops, got involved in student groups, drifted into the radical causes that swept the nation in the sixties.

At sixteen, Nile joined the Black Panther Party, a group that struck fear into the hearts of much of white America. But to Nile, the party was a family dedicated to helping their brothers and sisters help themselves. "They taught me the foundation of what I would become. They taught me how to run a business and how to be self-sufficient," he says.

That was when he discovered music. A neighbor was in a band, and she was looking for a guitar player. "I pretended I could play," he said. He got his maternal grandfather's acoustic guitar out of a closet and sat in on the band session, trying to force out of the instrument the notes that were in his head. The other musicians mocked him. "You said you could play," they taunted. "You've really got an inflated opinion of yourself."

The humiliation made him determined to learn to play the guitar, if only to show them that he could. "I didn't realize that I was doing something that would happen the rest of my life," he says. "It's what jazz musicians call separating the men from the boys. It's putting yourself in a position beyond your talent. It's going to the woodshed and living it."

His mother, on a trip back home, bought him his first real guitar, and his stepfather taught him how to tune it. He got a book of Beatles songs, and the first song he learned to play was "A Day in the Life."

"It was," he says, "magic."

Nile was active in supporting the city's teachers in their contract negotiations. In gratitude, teachers at the Manhattan School of Music and the Juilliard School, Manhattan's preeminent school for classical music, allowed him to attend classes even though he wasn't enrolled in either school. The teachers even allowed him to give a recital with other students at the New York Public Library for the Performing Arts in Lincoln Center. He played Bach. "I never graduated from high school, but I got a great education," he says.

Within a year, he was playing on *Sesame Street*. From then on, Nile Rodgers knew that he could always support himself with his music. Now it was just a matter of finding the right partners and the right sound to make his mark in the world.

The partner was Bernard Edwards, a bass player. They played together for half a decade before they brought it all together with the band called Chic and the song called "Dance, Dance, Dance (Yowsah, Yowsah, Yowsah)." What would make them influential far beyond the band was a discovery they made during a recording session when a technician told them to roll the bass line down to subsonic levels.

It hadn't been done before, and with good reason. Speakers weren't built to handle tones below hearing but not below sense, a level at which the beat interacts directly with the deepest parts of the human brain, where the primal beat of life is embedded.

"You don't have to intellectualize it," he says. "It's just there. Once we put that in our music, it changed the course of our lives. I'm not saying this egotistically, but we changed music."

Soon they were being copied everywhere. The band Queen took Chic's base line and used it for their hit "Another One Bites the Dust." The Sugar Hill Gang appropriated the same line to record what is generally recognized as the first rap album.

What Chic did was so seminal that one pop music encyclopedia compares Rodgers to rock legend Chuck Berry in his influence on modern music.

But all the while Nile was building such great success, he was falling further into the grip of the drugs and alcohol that had been carrying him for all those years.

It had been a sometime thing for him during his formative years, and there were periods when he did no drugs, no alcohol at all, just as there were periods when he either gave up or took up many things in the search for spiritual fulfillment—Hinduism, martial arts, celibacy, abstinence. Children of the sixties were like that, always searching for something better somewhere else.

For a long time, he lived with the demon drug and survived the fame and the traveling and money and the groupies and all the rest of the wild life that claimed so many of his peers.

"My shrink told me I was falling all that time, but I was falling forward," he says. Despite himself, he kept moving ahead.

I am often amazed at how strong the creative force really is and how powerfully we are driven by what we are inside. For many years, Nile was a productive and creative person. It took a long time for the alcohol and drugs to finally take command. The lesson isn't that you can perform despite it all, but that in the end the substances win.

When you fall for a career, it lifts you up. But when you fall for drugs, you crash. Says Nile, "I didn't have a big record for five or six years. Drugs and alcohol got me. Drugs were part of my entire existence."

As he descended he started to realize that it was a family disease. His father had died in his thirties of cirrhosis of the liver. "No one in my family ever died from anything but drugs or alcohol. I have a cousin in jail for inadvertently killing his girlfriend while he was on crack. I have another cousin who was sawed in half over drugs," he says, emphasizing that that is literally how his relative was killed. "My whole life revolved around drugs and alcohol. I was a drug addict of the biggest magnitude."

It took a long time to realize it, all the way from that therapeutic beer in 1977 to Madonna's birthday party in Miami Beach, Florida, in August 1994.

"I had my first bout of cocaine psychosis at her party," he says. "I had been doing drugs all my life with very few adverse effects." But he had never done anything seriously loony, never been a danger to himself or others, until that night.

During the party, he was doing coke and he started to believe everyone was out to kill him. "I talked to a bunch of my friends and they told me that was the coke talking to me, that I was suffering from cocaine psychosis."

He went back to his hotel and sat with the demons he knew were out to get him. He had a gun and a samurai sword. "I was ready to go out like Bruce Lee," he says. "I was insane and I knew it. I realized I had crossed the line."

He remembered reading a magazine article by Keith Richards, the guitarist for the Rolling Stones who was going through another stint in rehab, trying to kick his own habits. "What he said meant everything to me," Nile recalls. "He asked himself, could he live without music? The answer was clearly no. Could he live without drugs and alcohol? The answer was clearly yes. The drugs and alcohol were diminishing his ability to appreciate music, and music was and is my one true friend in life.

"It is the one thing that drew me back to reality."

That was, he says, "my second epiphany—my second Moment of Truth."

The love of music was the one thing that had been his friend and solace for his entire life, the thing that made him complete. Nile quit drinking and drugging that night—a Friday—and waited out the weekend in his hotel room. He flew back to his home in Connecticut on Monday and checked himself into a rehabilitation facility. He has not had a drink or taken an illegal substance since then, and his life has never been better.

He is building a resort hotel and recording complex in the Turks and Caicos Islands in the Caribbean; touring again with Chic; running his company, Sumthing Else Music Works; producing and performing music that is important to him.

He likes to tell the story about his first sober performance. A friend of his had died on a dance floor of a heart attack, the victim of a congenital heart defect that had gone undetected until it killed him. Chic played a benefit concert at the club where the friend died.

"That was the first time I got onstage without a drink," he says. "It was strange, and I was so scared. I started talking and I just became high off the music. When we were done, I said to the crowd, 'Wow! Thank you. I belong up here.' I was standing on the edge of the stage. The people didn't even know what I was talking about, but I didn't care. It was, 'Wow, this is where I belong.'"

BILL PARCELLS

If you measure success by the amount of money someone makes, then Bill Parcells is a very successful man. But he never set out to become rich. It is amazing how many financially successful people would tell you the same thing.

What Parcells and others like him know is that happiness doesn't come from a paycheck. It comes from doing what you truly enjoy doing, from doing the thing that makes you who you are. For him, that is being a teacher, which is how he describes his job. The facts that what he teaches is football and that he has done it extremely well have made his name a household word and have ensured that he is nearly certain to be inducted into the Professional Football Hall of Fame in the future. Bill's Moment of Truth came when he realized what made him happy and chose to do it. Everything else that followed was just a bonus.

It was a typical day in a typical week for Bill Parcells, which means that at 11 A.M. on an autumn day in 1999 he was sitting in a smallish room behind a small Formica-topped table with a microphone and twenty or thirty people in front of him. He was a football coach—some say the best in the business—and this daily half hour of feeding the media was part of every National Football League coach's job.

But to go to a Bill Parcells press conference and come away thinking that this is typical of such sessions with such coaches would be a mistake. Other coaches dispense information—who is injured, who has a particularly big challenge ahead, which lineup change to expect. Parcells teaches.

A lot of people miss that. They think coaching is all about X's and O's on a chalkboard, about strategy and schemes. But that's the least part of winning football games, which is why a lot of coaches with a lot of strategy floating around in their skulls never play for championships as Parcells seemed always to be doing.

The biggest part of the job is teaching players how to make all those diagrams work in the real world of dirt and grass and clashing pads and all the rest that is the controlled chaos of a football game. It's teaching receivers how to catch, blockers how to block, pass rushers how to evade blocks, defenders how to tackle, runners how to run. Most important, it's teaching regular players how to win, probing the psyches of human beings and finding the right buttons to push to make them better than they think they can be, to make them champions.

It's really no different from the job any teacher takes on. Teaching football is simply more public than teaching history or math. At bottom, though, success is measured by the teacher's ability to touch the student. That is also where the satisfaction comes from.

It's something that Parcells seems to have been born doing, something that he is unable to stop doing, even when he's facing a roomful of reporters who think they already know everything there is to know about the game.

On one particular morning in November 1999, someone asked him about Curtis Martin, the star running back on Parcells's New York Jet team, and how important Martin was to the team. "He's a character guy," Parcells said, in a voice grown increasingly growly over the years, the result of daily use at full volume. "The more character guys you have, the better off you are."

Just like that, everyone in the room had learned more about the game than if he had said, "He's a great running back." What has always intrigued Parcells is why people are what they are. Character ranks big in his value system. "Character guys" win football games. Guys who have a lot of talent but no character don't. As for running backs, there is more to it than gaining yards, he goes on. There's catching passes, blocking, and picking up blitzing linebackers trying to turn the quarterback into a pile of broken bones. You do all those things, he says, and you're a football player. "Otherwise, you're just a runner."

You could go to a year's worth of his press conferences, write down all the little lessons, of which there are half a dozen a day, and at the end of it have a pretty good book about coaching and winning. Every statement is a terse observation boiled down to its essence after nearly forty years of professional coaching.

Parcells seems to have been born to coach. Even as a kid, he not only played the games but coached them as well. There was the day in a Babe Ruth League baseball tournament when Parcells was the catcher and the team needed one out to win and he switched places with the left fielder, because he knew the batter was going to hit the ball there—and he did. Or the day on the football field when he was the quarterback and his high school team had one more chance to score and Parcells traded places with the halfback, took the ball, and scored.

This all happened in New Jersey, in the suburban towns of Hasbrouck Heights and Oradell, where he grew up.

"I knew he was going to be a coach," says Mickey Corcoran, who coached Parcells in high school basketball. "Anyone who hangs around the gym when he's fifteen years old every chance he gets obviously has some interest in coaching. He was a gym rat."

Duane William Parcells, born in 1941, was the oldest of Charles "Chubby" Parcells's four children, three of whom were boys, all of whom were athletes. He was the best on the field, and he won a scholarship to college to play football. No one ever called him Duane. In his family, he was Willie. In high school, he was Billy. Now, he's just Bill.

Parcells was a standout linebacker at Wichita State University, good enough to be drafted into the NFL when he graduated. But rather than play in the pros, Parcells went straight to the only job he ever wanted—coaching.

He started low on the coaching totem pole—as an assistant at Hastings College in Nebraska, then moved on to Wichita State, Army, Vanderbilt, Florida State, Texas Tech, and Air Force, where, in 1978, he first became a head coach.

He lasted only one year at Air Force, leaving of his own accord because he didn't like all the other things college coaches have to do in addition to coaching, including begging kids to come to their school. Besides, Parcells always had his eye on the pros. After quitting, he was offered a job as an assistant coach for the New York Giants. As a kid, he had worshiped the Giants. It had always been his dream to coach them.

So here he was with his dream job within his grasp. There was only one problem. He had convinced himself he couldn't take it.

Coaching had taken an enormous toll on his family. He had three daughters, of whom he saw little, and his many jobs had kept the family moving from one state to another, never staying anywhere long enough to put down roots. Bill's wife, Judy, was tired of the gypsy life, tired of never seeing him. She begged him to give up coaching, get a normal job, settle down and live like a normal family man.

He decided he had to do what she asked, if only to see whether he could. It was not an easy decision. What really is best for you and your family? Is it chasing your dream or sacrificing that dream for their interests?

Bill didn't know. That he was willing to put his family's needs first shows what kind of man he is. Many others wouldn't have considered giving up something they loved doing. But Bill felt he owed it to his family. He also thought he owed it to himself. Maybe he, too, would find the settled life more satisfying than the stomach-churning world of coaching.

He took a job selling real estate and stayed in Colorado. And, he says, "I was miserable."

In his line of work, there are Moments of Truth nearly every day. He has been to three Super Bowls and won two of them, and he has taken three teams to conference championship games. He has faced numerous must-win games, has nearly been fired, has had public battles with general managers and owners, has had a bout with heart disease and heart surgery. But if there was one Moment of Truth in Bill Parcells's life, it was the year that he tried to live a "normal life."

He made it through the year and watched his oldest daughter graduate from high school, but he wasn't content. There was no visceral thrill in selling real estate. Walking onto a lot with a client was no match for standing in the tunnel underneath a packed stadium before a game, listening to the roar of the crowd and feeling the butterflies in his gut, getting ready to take the field and do battle.

Coaching is hard on families—always has been, always will be. But *not* coaching was like a living death to Bill. If he stayed away from it, he wouldn't be a better family man. He would just be a more miserable person. Inevitably, his unhappiness would spill over into his family life.

Trying a different way taught him that. Because of that year, he could go back to coaching and give it everything he had. He knew better than anyone how important it was to him. Bill says he never regrets the year he took off. He learned too much about himself to regret it. And his family did not regret his return to coaching. They understood what it meant to him. In return, he gave them as much of himself as he could. If anything, the family became closer because of what they went through together.

It comes down to what he told reporters in 1998, when he was taking the Jets to the AFC Championship game and people were speculating that he was close to retirement. "I'm coaching," he told them with conviction. "I'm coaching as hard as I can. I'm committed."

It's how he felt in 1980, when he put real estate behind him forever and walked back onto a football field, coaching linebackers for the New England Patriots. A year later, he was running the defense for his hometown Giants. Two years after that, he was the head coach of the Giants.

He almost didn't have a chance to prove his worth. That first year, he went 3–12–1 and was within an eyelash of being fired. But the owners decided to give him another year, and he responded by taking the team to the play-offs in 1984. Two years later, he won the franchise's first Super Bowl, and four years after that he won another.

Bill quit after the second Super Bowl triumph, not because he had had enough of coaching, but because his coronary arteries were all but blocked and his heart couldn't take the stress of the sidelines. He underwent several angioplasties before finally resorting to coronary bypass surgery. He spent a year behind a microphone doing color analysis on television, but then he was back on the football field, teaching the New England Patriots, a team with a long history of failure, what it takes to win.

In Boston, he was viewed as a savior and treated like a

genius. He liked to tell people that coaching football, "ain't rocket science, you know. I'm just a regular guy. I've just been lucky. Things went well for me right from when I grew up."

He admitted that the best moments were on the practice field, where he could really coach. "The practice field is my sanctuary. It's what I enjoy about my job. It's the nuts and bolts of what I do. The games are a reflection of how well I did it."

Bill won't argue that he was paid extremely well for being just a teacher. But he also knows that his satisfaction has little to do with his paycheck.

"I just want to give these kids a chance to succeed," he often says. More often than not, they do that. He took the Patriots to the Super Bowl and almost beat the highly favored Green Bay Packers. Then he went to the New York Jets, whose history was as lackluster as any in the game. Within two years he had them playing for a championship.

Bill always said he'd quit when he couldn't give as much of himself as he asked of his players. After the 1999 season, he had reached that point and announced his retirement from the sidelines. His hair was whiter and the wrinkles on his face were deeper, but until his final game, the teacher inside him remained young.

Bill stayed on with the Jets as the general manager, and he finally had a little more time to give to his family. He had managed to keep following his dream, be a father and husband and help to raise three fine daughters. When he began his career, it was "my way." During his year in real estate, it was "her way." In the end, it became "our way."

CHRIS EVANS

Motivation, drive, ambition. Some people are born with these qualities. Others travel a long road before they discover them. This was true of my friend Chris Evans. Before his Moment of Truth, he wandered aimlessly through life, working at jobs not because he wanted to make something of himself but because he wanted the money to spend on a life of nightclubs and parties. His life changed when he learned that his father had lied to save himself the embarrassment of admitting that his son was wasting his life.

The first time I met Chris Evans I knew he was special.

I was working for Bloom Advertising in the late 1970s in Dallas, and my job took me out of town at least three times a week. I'd drive to the Dallas–Fort Worth Airport, go through the hassle of finding a parking place, stashing the car, catching the shuttle bus, dragging my baggage with me. It's not the easiest way to travel, but it never occurred to me to do it any other way.

One day my car was in the shop, and I had to get a ride. I told my secretary to call a cab, and Chris was the fellow who picked me up in a spotless yellow cab. I noticed he wasn't like other cabbies. He wore a shirt and tie, got the door for me, said, "Yes, sir" and "No, sir." He was so affable I couldn't resist talking to him during the ride. When he dropped me off, I got his name, and from that day on, I never drove myself to the airport again. When I had to catch a flight, I had my secretary call Chris.

Seeing each other as often as we did, we got to know one another, and not just in a cabbie-fare kind of way.

"We started being friends," is the way Chris puts it. "I mean real friends."

Over time, we traded life stories. He was born in 1957 in Marlin, Texas, south of Waco. His father, Wallace Evans, was a schoolteacher and a good one. He got to be principal of a school in Marlin at a time when few black men were leading schools that were primarily white. Chris was ten and too young to remember much, but he knows his father moved the family—Chris had a younger brother by then— to Dallas, Texas, after racists burned his school down.

Wallace Evans went right back to teaching at a middle school in Dallas. Just a year after the family moved, Chris's mother, Earlene, died of a heart attack. She was barely forty years old. Wallace raised his two sons himself for the next five years before he remarried.

Wallace wanted his sons to go to college, but Chris wasn't

fond of school. "I was a wild kid," he told me. So he took vocational classes in high school, dreaming of the day he would be on his own.

But being on your own and knowing what to do with that freedom and responsibility are different things. Like many kids, Chris hadn't given much thought to what he wanted to do with his life. Having a good time seemed enough.

Chris took a job with Control Data Corporation, but quit after less than a year. Then he went to a management school run by Arby's, the fast-food restaurant chain. Arby's sent him to San Antonio to manage a franchise. After a year and a half, the company transferred him to Dallas, where he worked for another year and a half, managing another restaurant.

In Dallas, Chris roomed with another young man who drove a cab and spent his free time and all of his spare money partying. When Chris's car broke down one day, he didn't have the money to fix it, so he bummed rides to and from work in his roommate's cab. This gave Chris an idea. Instead of worrying about getting rides to work, why not go into the cab business himself? That way, he'd always have a car.

Of such simple necessities are careers born.

So Chris went to Vernon Robinson, who owned the Yellow Cab that Chris's roommate drove. Robinson took Chris on as a driver. It was 1978. Chris was thirty-one years old. He had fathered a child but hadn't married the mother. And he still had no clear idea of what he wanted to do with his life.

He says he was wild and loved the nightlife and the ladies. But he was also inwardly torn because he was a good man liked by all who met him, a diligent and dependable worker. Robinson took a liking to him, too. The older man would invite Chris to sleep at his house after Chris got done driving his cab on the late shift. Within a year, Chris had decided to buy his own cab, and Robinson sold him one of his own.

From the outside, Chris's rise looks straightforward. He started small, built a clientele by word of mouth, turned his cab company into a limo service, got married, raised four children, became a minister in his church, and is now the owner of a fleet of vehicles. There's a temptation to remark on how lucky he's been.

But luck didn't have a great deal to do with it. And the road was hardly straight and smooth. A number of his friends didn't get anywhere, caught up in the shallow but glitzy life of clubs and drugs and, ultimately, failure. Chris readily admits he could have gone the same way.

In fact, for a while he was so uncertain about where he was headed that he quit driving a cab altogether and got a job in a Payless shoe store, supplementing his income by working in Dallas's hot clubs at night. As often as not, he sucked his paycheck up his nose. Cocaine was the "in" drug in those days. All the hotshot athletes and Hollywood stars were doing it. If it was good enough for them, it was good enough for Chris.

I think of that when I hear athletes say they have no desire to be role models. Whether they want to be or not, they are. And every time they get out of line, a lot of good people like Chris Evans follow them.

Chris admits, "I was just floating. I didn't know what I wanted."

By selling shoes, Chris learned that he preferred driving cabs, so he bought another car and went back into the business. But things were different now. A woman and a child were part of his life.

He met Regina, a strong and pious woman from Paris, Texas, in 1979 when she was visiting her sister in Dallas. The sister lived in the same apartment building as Chris, and Regina and Chris met when they were doing their laundry. She caught his eye immediately, and he did everything he could to impress her. "I was trying to be real fast and cool," he remembers, laughing at himself. Whatever he did, she noticed, and when he called her after she went home, she asked him to come up to meet her family, which included her three children.

When they finally married, they took in Chris's child from a previous relationship, and together they raised Yamica, Coco, Terence, and Camesha. But as much as he loved his wife and children, Chris couldn't commit himself to a life of responsibility. He was still a party animal.

One day, he got a letter from a professor and his wife who were lifelong friends of his father's. Chris's father had visited the couple in their home in a town outside of Dallas, and when they asked what Chris was doing, Wallace Evans said, "He's driving a limousine." In their letter to Chris, they asked about his job.

"It may seem insignificant to anyone else," Chris says,

"but that got me going. He didn't want to say his kid was a cab driver. I realized I hadn't lived up to his expectations and that he was embarrassed of me.

"If I had a Moment of Truth, that was it."

As a parent, I can understand how hard it would be to tell your child how disappointed you are. I can also understand how a child might realize the heartbreak he's causing those who love him. Sometimes it takes a third party relaying something said in innocence to make a person see. This was one of those times.

Holding the letter with the unintentionally damning words, Chris took stock of himself. "I looked at the money I was making—good money. But I didn't have any saved up. I was wasting it, living from day to day with nothing to show for my work. I realized I was heading nowhere, and I had a wife and children to care for."

The letter came at the same time that his wife was gently prodding him to come back to his religion. He went to church to keep her happy, but when he got the letter and had his transforming moment, he went because he wanted to. The wild kid became a sober, churchgoing businessman.

It all came together. Chris looked at the business he had begun to build—a good business. "And I realized I was wasting it all," he says. "One day I just threw the drugs away and I never went back." He replaced them with a Bible, which has traveled with him ever since, on the dashboard of his car.

Prodded by his father's words, he went to Earl Shibe, the economy paint-job place, had his yellow cab painted blue, and went into the limo business. "It wasn't a great paint job," he says now with a laugh. "You could see 'Yellow Cab' through the blue. People didn't know what they were riding in."

I had never known the true story behind Chris's success, despite all the time we'd spent together over more than twenty years. We all tend to hide the pain inside us.

Armed with his new sense of responsibility and his ambition to finally make something of himself, so that his father, his wife, his children, his pastor, and his Savior could all be proud of him, Chris bought another used town car, hired another employee, and kept building his business. He put the energy he had once put into partying into church and eventually became a minister himself. His relationship with his wife and family became deeper and more satisfying than he had ever imagined they could be. One of Chris's greatest joys was seeing his father's pride when Chris told him that he didn't have to lie anymore.

Chris was so successful he didn't even have an ad in the Yellow Pages until he had been in business for almost fifteen years. Yet among his corporate clients were Arthur Andersen Consulting, Mobil Oil, C.S. Wireless, McNeilus Trucking, and Hollywood Casino, all big businesses in Dallas. "I got all my business by word of mouth," he says.

I am proud to say I helped spread the good word about Chris, but I wasn't the only one. Anyone who has dealt with Evans Limousine has gotten the finest service available—anywhere. Even though Chris now devotes his time to managing the business and doesn't drive anymore, every one of his employees knows the company's motto, "Corporate

Friendly," and everyone knows how Chris Evans demands they conduct themselves.

"It takes some sacrifice," he says of the secret of success in his business. But, as he found out in his personal life, the rewards more than make up for it.

JAYSON WILLIAMS

The tragic loss of two family members left Jayson Williams angry at the world. His anger threatened to eat a hole in his soul. And his pain spilled over until it strained his family. When his father explained to him what he was doing, Jayson experienced his Moment of Truth. He took stock of himself, changed his ways, and began to heal. His story is a testament to the power of a son's love for his parents and of theirs for him.

It is Opening Day 1999 for the New Jersey Nets in the Continental Arena, and Jayson Williams, NBA All-Star, as perfect in his pin-striped suit as a swished three-pointer, is mingling with the pregame crowd. He's a center for the Nets, but it will be another year before all the damage inflicted on his body over the previous season—a broken leg, a bum knee, and torn ligaments in his thumb, all of which required surgery to repair—will be fully healed and he's on the court again. So he comes to the game, supports his teammates, does what he can to help.

He's tall and lithe and strong, with the kind of good looks that make women swoon and men wish they could spend just one day in his shoes. But none of that is what makes Williams stand out in a basketball arena. The hardwood is crowded with men like him.

Something else makes Williams special, and you see it immediately as he makes his way through a crowd, stopping for every person who wants an autograph, shaking hands, hugging friends, bending down to make a child laugh, giving a little bit of himself to everyone who asks, leaving a wake of smiles.

We'd like all athletes to be like this—approachable, affable, never in too much of a hurry to sign an autograph or say something nice to a fan, grateful for the fame and attention, appreciative of the great gobs of cash that are thrown at them. But expecting every athlete to be like that is like demanding that every dog be like Lassie. Life simply doesn't work that way.

"I've always had a good heart. I've never had any problems helping people," he explains, saying what everybody who has ever met him already knows. He only had problems helping himself. He's not alone in that. A lot of people find it easy to be nice to others but can't be that good to themselves.

Jayson grew up in a fine family. His father was a master mason, a man who took great pride in everything he did. And whatever his father did, Jayson wanted to do. So when

Jayson was just eight years old, his father took him to jobs and put him to work learning to lay brick.

The boy was bright and quick, but he also wanted everything to happen immediately. He would lay brick fast and furious, not bothering with the finer points, like keeping things square and level.

"My father used to say, 'Jayson, you know what? Look at this wall. Look how bad it is. You laid it in an hour, right? Now it's going to take you two hours to take it back down. If you take your time and do it right the first time, one right brick is better than two thousand wrong ones.' "

Jayson is thirty-one years old when he tells that story, and it is as if it were yesterday, as if he is still hearing his father's voice, still looking at the wall he built too fast.

He was an exuberant child, who wanted everything and wanted it now. Some people never grow out of that, and it spills over into whatever else they do. It was that way for Jayson, for whom a lot of things happened too fast, especially learning that the world is not always a neat and nice place. There is a lot of pain and personal tragedy in him that few people ever see behind his ready smile and the constant stream of jokes. Both have made him a hit on talk shows and with journalists who are grateful for the way he fills up their notebooks.

He was the clown, laughing on the outside, crying on the inside; the macho man, never letting them know he hurt. And the hurt went way back in his life.

The first blow landed when he was just twelve. He was the youngest child in a sprawling family that represented a lot of what's good about America. His father, E.J., an

African American, and his mother, Barbara, an Italian American, were both on their second marriages, and Jayson was the only child they had together. Then they adopted another child and brought ten children from their previous marriages to make a big, rambunctious family of twelve. They lived on the Lower East Side of Manhattan, and E.J. worked hard, managing not only his construction business but also a gas station he owned.

As the older children married, the extended family turned into what Jayson calls a mini United Nations, with Americans of Polish, Hispanic, African, and Italian ancestry descending on Barbara Williams's groaning table at Thanksgiving and other holidays.

The day everything changed began like any other for Jayson. When school let out—he was in the sixth grade—he walked the two blocks home, only to find the entry to the apartment building the family lived in crowded with police. He pushed his way inside and found his sister Linda covered with blood and beaten to a pulp in the hallway. Her assailant had stabbed the twenty-two-year-old woman fourteen times and beaten her with a hammer.

She didn't see the man and knew only that he had blood on his sneakers. Jayson grabbed a knife from the kitchen and burst back out of the building in a blind rage, running through the streets and parks, looking for a man with bloody sneakers. To this day, he is grateful he didn't find him, because if he had, Jayson knows he would have become a twelve-year-old murderer.

Linda, who had a two-year-old son named after her father, recovered. But in the hospital, she received a transfusion that was tainted with a relatively new virus that was just beginning to plague the world—HIV. Two years later she died of AIDS.

It was the kind of tragedy that wasn't supposed to happen to good people. And that was where Jayson's anger began, an anger that was all the worse because it had no identifiable object. Then, hard on its heels, more tragedy struck the family he treasured.

First, Jayson's mother took ill, contracting stomach cancer and a number of other illnesses. She was in and out of hospitals and underwent numerous operations when Jayson was becoming a basketball star at St. John's University in nearby Queens. Then, in his first year in college, another sister, Sissy, died of cirrhosis of the liver, leaving an orphan daughter, Monique.

Jayson undertook the care of both his sisters' children, who were now eight and ten years old. He got up early to get them to school, went to school himself, then often took them to basketball practice with him after classes.

Taking care of his nieces kept Jayson, who is more than a little rambunctious himself, out of serious trouble. But the anger and pain at a world and a God who could allow his sisters to die and his mother to be so ill festered inside him. He kept his feelings well hidden, but occasionally they would explode, as they did in Providence one night when a heckling fan became too much for him and he threw a chair at the offending party. On two other occasions, he was suspended for fighting.

But mostly, Jayson partied long and hard, medicating

the hurt inside with large doses of vodka and cranberry juice—his favorite potion.

He was making the mistake a lot of kids make, confusing an alcoholic haze with happiness, substituting a temporary anesthetic for real healing.

After he graduated and was drafted by the Philadelphia 76ers in 1990, he legally adopted his sisters' children and took them to live with him. Today, both E.J. and Monique are in their twenties, with children of their own, and Jayson laughs about becoming a grandfather before he was thirty. Jayson took his responsibilities as a father seriously, but after he was drafted and had money to hire full-time care for them, he found he still had time to party. The nightlife took its toll on the basketball court, where he did not live up to the potential he had shown in college.

After two years, the 76ers traded him to the New Jersey Nets. He was close to home, but he was not enjoying professional basketball, despite the fine life it afforded him. He found himself wishing he were still in college, where his St. John's coach, Lou Carneseca, treated his players like family. And family was important to Jayson.

In the pros, every player was responsible for himself. If he didn't want to put in the effort and the time and to cultivate good habits, they would find someone who would.

"Lou Carneseca was the kind of guy who made sure you got your sleep, made sure you got something to eat, did what you're supposed to do," Jayson says. "I came into the NBA, and it was just a business, and I didn't like that. I wanted it to be more than that. I wanted to be around St. John's more than I wanted to be around here."

His first year with the Nets, 1992–93, he did no better than he had in Philadelphia. Most of his antics were just kid stuff, done without malice. But in January 1994 he went over the line.

He and several friends left Continental Airlines Arena at two in the morning after a game that had ended hours earlier. They had been drinking, and one of Williams's friends asked to see the gun that Williams, like many professional athletes, kept in his car. Instead of just looking at the .40-caliber weapon, the friend fired it into the tire of a truck parked in the lot.

The next day, when the owner of the truck filed a complaint, Williams confessed. To protect his friend, he said he had fired the gun, which he had a license to own but not to carry. He was criminally charged for not having a permit and for illegally discharging it. He was put in a pretrial intervention program and ordered to perform community service.

The real punishment came when Williams had to face his father. "That was when my father sat me down and said, 'You know, your mom's got Parkinson's disease. You have your kids that you adopted, and you're setting a bad example,' " Jayson says.

"He said, 'Everybody knows you got a good heart, but what kind of jerk goes shooting a gun off in a parking lot?' "

Jayson explained that he didn't shoot the gun. "I don't care if it wasn't you," his father said. "You shouldn't have had a gun in your truck."

Barbara Williams was in the room, and when Jayson

looked at her, he knew how badly he had hurt both his parents. "I always wanted to bring them joy," he says. "That was the time my father said, 'Well, are you going to get your ducks in a row? If not, why don't you just quit and come and work construction?' "

"It was killing my parents," Jayson says. Not just the gun, but all the partying he was doing, all the talent he was throwing away. "My father was looking older and older. He had watched me party for four years. He said, 'Okay, we gave you four years of acting up and cutting up because of your sisters. Enough of that crap now. We're all suffering. You need to get yourself back together and quit blaming your behavior on everyone else.' "

Then his father said the words that cut through Jayson like a knife: "I'm disappointed in you."

"When your father looks you in the eye and says that, it hurts," Jayson says. "I'd rather take a beating. Just beat my butt, but don't tell me you're disappointed in me. Those are the things that changed my life around, and it changed it around for the best.

"I changed my life," he goes on. "I've always had a good heart. I was just so angry at the world for taking my sisters. It took me a long time to overcome that."

That was Jayson Williams's Moment of Truth, the moment when he began to be not just a great talent but a great human being.

The next year the Nets got a new coach, Butch Beard. For the first time, a pro coach took Jayson aside and said, "Look, you're part of my family."

Then assistant coach Paul Silas, a big man who had been

a ferocious rebounder during his days on the court, took Jayson on as a project. It had become apparent by then that Jayson was not going to be a great scorer. But he was tough and intense. If he could learn a special skill, his future in the league would be secure.

"I want you to try to rebound," Silas told Jayson. "You're not going to be the kind of all-star who's going to be a shooter. You're going to have to learn to do one thing in this league that nobody else can do."

Says Jayson, "These two guys took me under their wing, especially Paul. Paul would call me every night and make sure I was home, and I was home."

He says that simply getting older helped a lot. "Drinking vodka and cranberry until four o'clock in the morning—you can do that when you're twenty-two. You get to be twenty-seven, twenty-eight years old, gee, you feel like you've been drinking for two or three days. I just couldn't do it."

Or, as Willis Reed, a Hall of Fame center with the Knicks who became an executive with the Nets, told Jayson, "You can't hang out with the owls and soar with the eagles."

Jayson became one of the best rebounders in the NBA, which is to say, in the world. He made the All-Star team, and his inability to pass a kid who wants an autograph without signing made him one of the most popular players the Nets had ever had. The Nets rewarded his loyalty and his skills with a multimillion-dollar contract, and he designed and built his dream house in New Jersey. He and his father helped lay the brick for it. He fell in love and got engaged and now spends his evenings at home, where he knows he belongs.

He will never stop grieving the death of his sisters, but he now knows that it is better to honor their memories by being a good citizen than to nurse his anger at their deaths. His parents set a high standard for him when he was growing up, and he knows how lucky he is that they loved him enough to tell him when he disappointed them as an adult. Most of all, Jayson Williams knows now that his problems weren't with the world or with God, but with himself.

PART FOUR

Small Steps Can Bring You to a Moment of Truth

Some people experience a Moment of Truth when they set an ambitious goal and go after it in small, incremental steps. Their progress might seem negligible, too gradual to be noticed. But eventually they're often amazed by how much they've accomplished. And, in the process, they not only achieve success beyond their wildest hopes, they also discover that they've changed their lives, become better people, and found a fulfillment they didn't know was possible.

I have a friend who, when people bemoan the enormous task in front of them, asks, "Is it the mountain in front of you, or the mountain you put in front of you that's holding you back?" It is an excellent question. When the mountain is there, you can plan a way around it. When you put it there, an obstacle of your own making, it can become an insurmountable barrier.

I'm also reminded of the old joke: When you're up to your

armpits in alligators, it's hard to remember you're supposed to be draining the swamp. It is at such times that attending to the details—the alligators—is all you can do, but if you do that successfully, in the end you may just find that you've also drained the swamp.

Don Fink is one of the best Ironman triathletes in the world, but when he started the sport, he wasn't good enough to place in the smallest amateur competitions. He could set goals but had no idea how to achieve them. When he realized that improvement takes place incrementally rather than all at once, he achieved greatness.

Father Ted Hesburgh was the president of the University of Notre Dame during the most contentious and revolutionary years of modern history. While building Notre Dame into one of the premier universities in the country, he also served on national and international commissions, dealt with campus protests, and still had time to talk to any student who knocked on his door. Yet he never seemed overwhelmed. During those years, he faced many Moments of Truth, but because he tackled each job step by step, he never felt he had a difficult decision to make. His achievements were truly built bit by bit.

Finally, there is Walter Anderson, the editor of Parade *magazine. He set out in life knowing that he wanted to be more than what his parents expected, but he had no idea how to accomplish that. He took one positive step, which led to another and another and another. Today, even he is amazed at how far he has come.*

DON FINK

He calls it "The One Percent Solution," and he discovered it by accident. But it has changed Don Fink's life and, through him, is changing the lives of everyone with whom he comes in touch. The path to the solution began with his desire to make something of himself. He found the answer—and his Moment of Truth—in the most insignificant of actions, proving that a journey of a thousand miles really does begin with a single step.

It is a given that there is no such thing as an easy triathlon, a sport that involves swimming, biking, and running. That said, some triathlons are less challenging than others, and as triathlons go, the one Don Fink was contemplating wasn't much, just a genial splash, ride, and jog for weekend athletes in Seaside Heights, on the Jersey Shore.

Yet Don stood on the starting line on this sunny afternoon in 1992 with more than the usual prerace jitters, for he had chosen this race to be the one in which he intended to prove himself worthy. A top-three finish was his goal—one that would put him on the victory stand and earn him a trophy, one that would show that he wasn't in sports what he was in everything else—a mediocrity.

Don was thirty-four years old and, as far as he could see, going nowhere. "Pathetic" is the word he uses to describe his accomplishments until then—"athletically, socially, and in business. I had not distinguished myself in any way.

"I had a relatively low management job with four people working for me—kind of a player-coach," he says, embarking on a litany of inadequacy. "I'm kind of embarrassed to even talk about it. I was very timid. I was terrified of public speaking. I went to meetings, hoping no one would call on me.

"I was an unsuccessful manager at a low level, with no idea what to do. I was afraid of flying, which doesn't help in business. In the triathlon I was afraid of sharks and would have panic attacks in the water, afraid I wouldn't make it to shore. I had every phobia you could think of."

In school, Don had been an average student and a second-string athlete. He grew up in a military household with a strict father who preferred that children be seen and not heard. Maybe that's how he came to be so timid, so afraid to speak up. Maybe his father's demand for perfection was why he slid so far into imperfection. Whatever the reason, he was what he was, and he didn't like it.

At least Don knew that much. The first part of becoming something better is understanding that you can't change the past. Few of us escape childhood unscarred. It is one thing to confront the past in an effort to find healing. But dwelling on it and blaming what *was* for what *is* never takes us forward. And Don knew he wanted to go forward.

Don's wife, Melanie, was a good athlete. She suggested triathlons. "I did it because of her," Don says. But Don had lived with his feelings of inadequacy for so long that they were ingrained. He worked out and practiced, but his efforts did not result in success. "I did all the things to be good," he says, "but was having no success."

Finally he decided to make one last mighty effort to get on the victory stand as a top-three finisher, and he chose the 1992 race to do it. He trained harder than he ever had in his life, was determined to finally succeed at something.

Don gave everything he had that day and finished exhausted. When he looked at the results for his age group, 30–35, he saw that he had finished eighth. "I had given it my all and my all was only eighth," he says. "I was unhappy with how I had done in many different areas, but I thought I would at least have some modest success, and even that didn't work. I was going to quit triathlons."

In this depressed state Don drove home, went to bed, and arose the next day to begin another week of work as the same-old-Don-Fink, Mr. Average. Life continued, but not any more merrily than before. Two weeks went by before he came home one night, picked up the mail, and sat down at the kitchen table to see what new bills the mail carrier had brought.

He came to a letter from the Seaside Heights Triathlon. Inside were the detailed results of the race. He opened the envelope without enthusiasm, found his name on the enclosed sheet, still in eighth place, and stared at it.

"I was kind of depressed, kind of worn-out," Don remembers. "What am I going to do next?" he asked himself. He read the names of the people who beat him. "It's not like the seven guys ahead of me were anyone anybody ever heard of," he says. "I scanned up to number three and saw a time. I had tried so hard to get up there. I wondered how much I missed third place by. It was a minute-forty."

Don had a calculator and, out of curiosity, ran the numbers to see how much better third place was than his time as a percentage. "It came up exactly one percent," he says.

Doodling on the calculator, Don had no real purpose in mind. But we don't always know what insignificant moment in life will turn out to be the one that changes everything. For Don, this was that moment. This was his Moment of Truth.

"Wow!" he thought. He didn't have to improve much at all to get on that victory stand. He just needed to improve his time by one lousy percent. But how?

Instead of thinking there were too many things he needed to do, he focused on three that looked the most promising. Then, knowing that the best of us need help, he got a coach and threw himself back into the sport. The improvement was immediate, so he started working on a couple more things on the list and got even better.

"Then it became a habit," he says. "It spilled over into

other areas of my life." He had no trouble thinking of something else on which to use his one percent solution.

He had stumbled on a formula that was about to change his life.

"Public speaking was an area in which I needed to get better just to survive," he says. "I started with a team meeting—just four people. I would overprepare the heck out of it. I'd do the presentation in front of the mirror all weekend. I prepared to an embarrassing level.

"I figured if I had an anxiety attack, I knew the speech so well, I could do it anyway on autopilot. That gave me confidence, and it worked. I was successful at a low level, but it was success. I started looking for an opportunity to give a public speech at a slightly higher level. When I had success at that, I looked for the next step up."

He applied his new technique to his fear of flying, to his fear of swimming, to everything. Little by little, Don Fink stopped being mediocre and became an achiever. He started rising up the ranks, not only in the world of triathlons but also at work. Every time he improved, he looked for another way to get a tiny bit better.

Now he was helping Melanie to improve as well. The pupil was becoming the teacher. Within a couple of years, Don had worked his way from small triathlons to the verge of the sport's biggest stage—the Ironman Triathlon, the ultimate test, consisting of a 2.5-mile swim, a 112-mile bike race, and a full 26.2-mile marathon.

When he started on his program, he says, "I never thought I would even go and see the Hawaii Ironman. Didn't even think I could do an ironman. It was just a step forward, just saying, 'I think I can make things a little bit better.' It was a couple of years before I was able to even run an ironman."

And when he did that, he set his sights on getting into the most famous race in the sport—the Hawaii Ironman, the race he never thought he'd see.

There are qualifying races for the Hawaii Ironman, which is the world championship race. The sweet irony was that the qualifier nearest him was held in Seaside Heights, New Jersey, the same venue at which he had first tried, and failed, to finish in the top three. The race was stretched to a half-ironman, and this time Don didn't settle for eighth, or even third. "I won it," he says. "That was the first time I won my age group, the first time I qualified for the world championships. I did it in the exact same place where I had my major failure."

Anyone who has triumphed at a scene of previous failure knows how sweet that moment can be. Especially for an athlete, few experiences match it.

He went to Hawaii, and he's been going back ever since. By 1998, Don Fink, former average athlete and professional nobody, was the top-ranked American in the sport in his age group and second in the world. He runs the Hawaii Ironman, Ironman Europe, and has branched out to Ironman New Zealand. The man who was barely a household name in his own household is now known by everyone in his sport.

He also became an eager flier and now travels everywhere. The man who was afraid to speak in public has addressed crowds of eight hundred people.

No longer an unsuccessful manager, he has thirty people working for him at Citigroup. "It's the largest financial institution in the world," he says. "I'm managing director of Citibank's Mid-Atlantic region. I'm also the supervisory principal for Citicorp Investment Services, a broker-dealer. My third responsibility is as Segment Champion for active investors, people with a net worth of $25 million or more; people with art holdings, personal aircraft, expensive homes in several locations."

Once, he comanaged four people. Now he advises the megarich.

When Citibank ranked its managing directors in 1997, Don was number one. "Our team is the role model for the United States," he says.

He himself is astonished by how far he has come, because he never set out to be the best, just to get better, one percent at a time. If ever there was a testament to conquering obstacles little by little, he is it.

"A by-product of all this is that I've also become financially well off. I don't need to work anymore, and I'm thinking about ending my business career. What I want to do now is mentor other people. I believe true success comes when you help other people. That's going to be my next project."

Don has become a certified personal trainer, and he also helps other triathletes follow the same road he took.

Along the way he has learned a great deal about life and about himself. "I used to feel that I just wasn't one of those people who have natural ability," he says. "I reject that now. I don't think anything is natural. It's just this concept

of 'Are you 100 percent good? Have you absolutely ful-
filled all of your potential?' You can't say yes. Can you get
one percent better? Of course you can. And you can do it
in everything.

"Here I am, one of the top master athletes in the world,
and I can be better."

He knows now that it comes down to how you view
yourself. "If you see yourself in a certain way, the world
sees you that way too. It really is true," he says. "So much
of it is mental. It was just impossible to stand on that beach
in Seaside Heights and think I could compete in an ironman on a national level. It was too much of a mega-mega
jump. It was too intimidating.

"But if you look at it as incremental, almost anything is
possible."

THEODORE M. HESBURGH, C.S.C.

⟨≈⟩

Father Ted doesn't think he's ever faced a transforming moment, which is just one of the many reasons why I find his story so inspiring. His example shows that Moments of Truth need not be overwhelming instants, burned into our memories forever. Father Ted tackles challenges by examining the subject from all sides, giving his prodigious intellect a chance to work, and then calling on his personal guide, the Holy Spirit, to help lead him to the truth. His abiding faith that the Spirit will guide him unerringly has allowed him to face the many major decisions of his long and distinguished career with quiet confidence and equanimity. His life is an example to us all.

To thousands of students, for the thirty-five years that he was president of the University of Notre Dame, he was simply "Father Ted." The nickname belied the enormous moral, intellectual, and spiritual stature of Theodore M. Hesburgh, a handsome and articulate leader who, more than any other one person, was responsible for transforming a small sectarian university with a big football team into a major center of higher learning.

From the time he was six years old, he never wanted to be anything other than a priest, and when he retired in 1987, that is what he considered himself to be—just a priest. But seldom has "just a priest" had such an impact on American society. Father Ted was an adviser to seven presidents and several popes, served on countless boards and commissions, stood at the center of the maelstrom that marked the Vietnam War, and, when the smoke had cleared, found himself listed in the *Guinness Book of Records* for receiving more honorary academic degrees than anyone in the world.

To hear him tell his own story, it happened in the natural flow of his life. "I don't really think of a Moment of Truth," he says today. "My life's been fairly steady. The best thing I did was join the Congregation of the Holy Cross and become a priest. It was very normal."

And yet, as I see it, Father Ted's life has been full of Moments of Truth. He protected both his campus and the rights of antiwar activists, stood up to President Richard Nixon and the Vatican, headed the U.S. Commission on Civil Rights and the U.S. Amnesty Commission, and even dared to declare that academic excellence was more important to Notre Dame than a great football team.

Few would call the many decisions he faced easy. That

he does is a testament to the powerful role that faith plays in his life.

The lesson he gives us lies in the way he faced these many crises with such self-assurance, in the way he regularly made decisions that affected the future of a great institution with calm logic. Father Ted showed that a Moment of Truth need not be gut-wrenching; that the *process of* making a decision with far-reaching ramifications can make the decision itself an anticlimax.

Davy Crockett, the legendary frontiersman who died at the Alamo, used to say, "Be always sure you're right—then go ahead." It's a pretty good description of how Father Ted made his own decisions. "You wait, and at a certain time, you go" is how he puts it.

"I think we all have to be open to movements of the Spirit," he says. "I think it's the Spirit that brings us the Moment of Truth. When we listen to the Spirit, we not only get the idea, but we also get the strength to do it."

He seemed to be born with the rare certainty of purpose that often marks great leaders. It showed itself early, when he decided so young to become a priest and stuck to that determination, even as he dated and went to dances and played sports through high school in the early 1930s. A visiting priest from the Congregation of the Holy Cross—the teaching and missionary order that founded and ran the University of Notre Dame—captured his imagination while Father Ted was an altar boy in his hometown of Syracuse, New York. When it came time some years later to enter the seminary, he'd already decided he would go to Notre Dame.

Becoming a priest, he says, was not a difficult decision in

those days. Vocations were still common, and a boy choosing the priesthood was not considered odd or different, as he might be today. The pressures to be worldly were not nearly as great.

At Notre Dame, he was marked early as a leader. The congregation sent him to study in Rome, but when World War II broke out, they brought him back to the States to complete his studies for his doctorate and the priesthood in Washington, D.C. The war years were a time of great responsibility but also of great opportunity for people in all walks of life, no less the priesthood. With a shortage of manpower everywhere, Father Ted found himself thrown again and again into one fray or another, with the freedom to do what he felt needed to be done.

Back at Notre Dame after the war, he rose rapidly through the ranks of his religious order until, at the age of thirty-two, he was named executive vice president of the university. Three years later, in 1952, he was its president, a post he would hold for the next thirty-five years. It was a time of unparalleled growth and maturation for Notre Dame. His goal when he took office was simple: to create from the raw clay of Notre Dame the greatest Catholic university in the world.

Father Ted began his work at Notre Dame with a simple directive from his predecessor, Father John Cavanaugh. "You don't make a decision because it's going to be popular," Cavanaugh told him. "You make a decision because you think it is right."

Initially, many things he did were very unpopular. Turning Notre Dame into a major institution of higher learning meant that many department heads, faculty members, and even students would have to go. Some of the people he fired or reassigned were his good friends, but Father Ted believed in his mission, and he did what he thought was right.

His actions required enormous courage, but to him there was no other way to go. So decisions that would be agonizing for others were not so for him. Although he grieved deeply to tell people they no longer fit in, his belief in what he was doing would not allow him to compromise.

As he became involved on national boards and commissions, he came to spend many days away from the campus. A popular saying of the time asked, "What is the difference between God and Father Hesburgh?" The answer: "God is everywhere. Father Hesburgh is everywhere except Notre Dame."

When he was on campus, the light in his office burned until the wee hours of the morning. As he worked into the night, he always left his office door open, and he never turned away a student who came to talk with him, no matter what the hour.

Once, when asked how he managed to handle so many tasks at once, he said, "You concentrate your fullest attention on one job while you are doing it, you do the best you can, and then you go on to the next one. When I have said or done something, it is over; I don't worry about it anymore. I doubt that I have spent more than half a dozen sleepless nights in my life. I put my worries aside. I say my prayers and go to sleep."

In the late 1960s that philosophy would be tested to the

utmost. During that period of campus ferment and antiwar activism, Father Ted faced several crises. One arose when the CIA and Dow Chemical, manufacturers of the napalm dropped on Vietnam, came to recruit among the senior class. Student activists vowed to sit down in front of the offices in which the interviews were taking place to block access by other students.

Father Ted actively opposed the Vietnam War, but he also believed that students who wished to interview for jobs should be allowed to do so. Even a closely held belief did not allow him to abridge the rights of others. So he clearly defined a policy under which protestors would be warned to clear the entrances to the offices. If they refused, they would be suspended from school for a year. And that is what he did.

Father Ted's strength in the face of student unrest earned him a congratulatory message from President Nixon, who invited him to Washington to help persuade a gathering of state governors to support national legislation to crack down on campus protestors. In an eloquent letter, Father Ted declined, arguing that the nation's universities didn't need more federal intervention, but less.

Through those difficult days, Father Ted was never motivated by political expediency but by fairness and compassion. He did not remain Nixon's friend, but the students, who at one time saw Father Ted as part of the problem, came to embrace him as standing on the side of justice.

Father Ted dealt with the Vatican in the same way. On several occasions during his presidency of Notre Dame, conservatives in the Church hierarchy attempted to limit academic freedom at Catholic universities, and Father Ted fought them off, knowing that without freedom there cannot be a university.

"It was never very agonizing," he says now of the many far-reaching decisions he made during his long and distinguished career. "I left it to the inspiration of the Holy Spirit."

But simple faith wasn't enough. Father Ted could rely on the Holy Spirit because he brought his intellect to bear on every problem he took on. He thoroughly thought out everything he did. And he had a strong sense of justice that was not dependent on the rote pronouncements of ideologues. If you have strong core values, and if you investigate a problem as thoroughly as is humanly possible, then the right path does become clear.

He explains the process as simply as he has lived his life. "When you know you need help, you ask for inspiration," he says. "You are given the light, and you go."

Wise words from a wise man.

WALTER ANDERSON

~

He was a tough kid. But as much as he excelled at fighting and hanging out, Walter Anderson had a gnawing feeling that there was more to life than his circumstances had allowed him to experience. He found hope in the love of a kindly woman who taught school. He found his Moment of Truth and his future through the U.S. Marine Corps. Sometimes that's all it takes, a place where you are accepted and an opportunity to try something new.

One thing Marine recruits don't usually have trouble doing is sleeping. But on this night, even a day of brutal physical exercise couldn't still Walter Anderson's churning seventeen-year-old mind. In the middle of the night he got up and softly paced the barracks, which was filled with the snorts and snores and sighs of sleeping men. In a little less than four years he would be out of the Corps. He would be twenty-one, an adult. What would he do then?

Walter slipped quietly back into his bunk under the Marine-issue olive blanket. There in the dark, surrounded by dozens of men and yet totally alone, Walter cried. He cried for himself, for his violent childhood, for his dreams, for his future. And he cried for every kid who has grown up wanting to make something of himself in an environment where success is not encouraged.

He had quit high school when he was sixteen years old. One of the career options open to him was crime. He thought about it. In the unforgiving neighborhood in Mount Vernon, New York, in which Anderson grew up, a lot of kids chose the path that led to Rikers Island, New York City's infamous jail, and then to Sing Sing or Attica.

Walter didn't go that way because, he says, deep down inside, "I wanted pride. I wanted to believe in something."

He told me this in a conference room in the midtown Manhattan offices of *Parade* magazine, of which he is the editor. The magazine is delivered with nearly every Sunday newspaper sold in America and is read by tens of millions of people.

If this were all he had become, it would be enough in the eyes of most people. But it is only part of Walter's extraordinary résumé. The high school dropout has been the valedictorian of two colleges, was the managing editor of a major suburban newspaper chain at the age of twenty-seven, has written four books, authored and starred in a one-man stage play, taught journalism, and teaches a confidence course. He's spoken to 300,000 people assembled in front of the Lincoln Memorial in Washington, D.C., written PBS specials, was awarded a Horatio Alger Award by Dr. Norman Vincent Peale, and counts among his close friends the likes of Nobel Prize–winning author Elie Wiesel, Bill Bradley, and Jerry Lewis. Did I mention that he has also raised millions of dollars for charity?

Walter is also my friend, and I am proud to be able to say that. He is someone I draw inspiration from, someone who proves that even if you're down, you're not necessarily out.

It all began that night in the barracks when the youth he was came face-to-face with the man he would become.

I would call it a Moment of Truth. Walter calls it by a different name. "I never felt there were turning points in life," he says. "But at certain times we are presented with an opportunity and we are ready for it and we transform ourselves. And human beings *can* transform themselves. I'm a living example."

After that long night in Parris Island, Walter went to his drill sergeant.

"What do you want, Anderson?" the sergeant asked.

"I want to go to school," the young marine responded.

Those words had never come out of his mouth before. As a kid, school was where he went to screw up and screw off. That's what he was expected to do, especially what his father expected him to do.

According to Walter, his father was a violent drunk, consumed by rage, haunted by demons. It maddened the father to see his son trying to make something of himself. Why should the kid be any better than the old man? Walter's father was illiterate, and if he came home from the local gin mill and found his son reading a book, he would savagely beat the boy.

Despite that, Walter's mother encouraged him to read. He loved books, but it didn't make sense to read them, knowing what would happen if his father caught him. So he asked his mother why he should risk the beatings and keep reading.

"So you can find your way out," his mother said.

Of all the words she said, those were the truest and they were filled with all the love she had. She knew she was stuck, but her son didn't have to be. Someday he would be old enough to read without worrying about being caught doing it. Someday, he wouldn't have to answer to a drunk. Someday . . .

So Walter became two people. One was the kid who had to be tougher, more profane, and wilder than every other kid in the neighborhood. The other was the one who took refuge in the still and quiet of the local library, reading books and magazines, dreaming of being the editor of *Life* magazine, of writing a novel.

One of his friends, Barry Williams, was the son of a teacher. Mrs. Ilza Williams had a master's degree from Columbia University, and her backyard was the neighborhood gathering place, a refuge for kids like Walter.

Ilza Williams knew Walter's home life wasn't out of *Father Knows Best*. She would find reasons for the boy to sleep over with her son, excuses for him to have a normal night in a loving home. She could tell that Walter was exceptionally bright, and she encouraged him to read and to do his homework.

So Ilza Williams, a black educator, took Walter Anderson, a white hellion, under her wing. She had him tested and confirmed what she knew about his great ability. Convinced that the public schools were not a place where he could flourish, she placed him in a parochial school. He got thrown out.

Undaunted, Williams sent him to another school. He entered as an eighth grader in September and left after finishing ninth grade the following June.

When he finished two class years in one school year, Williams was convinced of his intelligence and ability. She got him a scholarship to Westminster Prep, a prestigious Connecticut school that fed students to Harvard and other Ivy League schools. But when she took Walter there on a visit, he looked around and realized he would never fit in. The top-notch school was too frightening, so Walter didn't even try.

"I greased my hair back. I wore motorcycle boots," he says. "I dressed different. I talked different. I had an inferiority complex bigger than the State of New York, and I knew I didn't belong there."

Instead of telling Mrs. Williams that—he knew she would never accept it—Walter told a lie. "You can trust me," he told her. "I want to go to public school with my friends. I want to do well now."

The truth was he had no chance of doing well. Inside, he still felt worthless, still felt like the loser he was supposed to be.

His feelings were confirmed when he was fifteen years

old and actually wrote a novel that he sent out to publishers. When it was rejected, he threw it away in disgust.

Within a year and a half, he was failing nearly every subject. One of his teachers brought him to a guidance counselor. The teacher had no idea of the dreams and aspirations inside the boy. She just knew he was a terrible student. Together with the counselor, she encouraged him to enroll in a vocational program.

"What?" Walter remembers saying. "You think I'm a dummy?"

"No," she said, as if she were talking to a dummy. "I want you to show everyone how smart you are by going into a vocational program."

Walter was sixteen years old and if that was what they thought of him in school, he would simply quit. He went to the nearest recruiting office and joined the Marines.

I would call it another Moment of Truth. He had done his best to seem a dummy, but when confronted with the actual charge by someone, he took action. Behaving like a hoodlum wasn't the same as being one. And Walter knew he wasn't what he was pretending so hard to be.

He also understood he couldn't change where he was. He had to go somewhere new, somewhere fresh, where everyone started out equal. The Marine Corps was perfect.

As soon as he turned seventeen he enlisted and went to boot camp. That was in September 1961. "I wasn't going toward something as much as I was running away," he says. "And every other boot was just like me."

For Walter, that South Carolina autumn marked the

conjunction of opportunity and desire. Chances had been presented to him before, but now he was ready.

"If ever there were a transforming experience, that is the one time my life was transformed," he says. "That is where my life truly began. At [boot camp on] Parris Island, I learned pride, ethics, responsibility, a work ethic, spirituality, courage. That's where I was forged."

He remembers the first time he saw the obstacle course. It is a long, brutal, daunting beast, a monster that looks unconquerable. But the drill sergeant didn't call it an obstacle course. He called it a confidence course, and he promised every recruit that he would do it before he graduated.

The idea that difficulties are not obstacles but opportunities and confidence builders was new to Walter. And when he learned he could do the obstacle course, he learned he could do other things too. He could get the education he had so recently rejected.

He learned, in his words, that "confidence is an attitude, and attitudes are learned."

I hear that and I think of the attitude popular in many quarters that the American military is an evil institution. Nothing could be farther from the truth. For countless kids like Walter, it offers an opportunity to prove yourself. It is a meritocracy. You get out what you put in.

Walter told the sergeant he wanted to go to school, and the Marines arranged for him to take get his GED. He took the test and passed it at a very high level. When the Marines saw his score, they assigned him to electronics school in San Diego.

Just a year earlier, he would not have made it. Every

other marine in the school was a high school graduate and had either attended or graduated from college. "I had no confidence," Walter recalls. "No idea of math or algebra. But they told me, 'You can do this.' "

And he remembered that someone else had told him he could do it—Ilza Williams. "I realized that an educated person had believed in me," he says. "Even if I let her down, I thought that maybe that realization would get me through one day."

Here is proof that love is not wasted, even if when first offered it does not seem to find a home. You never know when the things you do for young people will take hold. That's why women like Mrs. Williams must never stop reaching out.

Bolstered by her belief in him, Walter vowed to get through just one day of school. That was all he wanted. To make it through one day of electronics school. So he made it through one day, and then one more, and by the end of the year, he had taken three courses and had graduated seventh out of twenty-four students.

Normally, the Marines promoted the top three students to lance corporal. The promotions were handed down by a faceless and nameless panel of officers. When the panel looked at where Walter had come from and where he had gotten to, they promoted him, the seventh-best student, as well.

"Anything I have ever achieved was not as large as the day those anonymous officers promoted me to lance corporal," Walter says. "They said, 'We believe in you.' That was a transforming experience."

Walter went to Vietnam and stayed in the Corps for five years. Jobs were tight, and being a veteran was, if anything, a mark against him with personnel directors. But he landed a job at a research lab where one day a middle-aged scientist called him "boy."

"Please don't call me that," said Walter, a combat-hardened man of twenty-two. The scientist thought the protest was funny and called him "boy" again.

More than thirty years later, Walter thought back on that moment and said it might qualify as a Moment of Truth because, he said, "I didn't coldcock the guy." Instead, he resigned.

In his desperation to get another job, he considered eliminating all references to the Marines and Vietnam from his résumé. As he thought about it, "I had a defining moment," he says. "I was walking down Fifth Avenue, considering taking Vietnam out of my résumé. And I was ashamed of what I was thinking. I decided that the first thing I would tell anyone who interviewed me was: 'Sergeant. Vietnam. U.S. Marines.' I would set an example for everyone like me for the rest of my life."

I suggest that everyone underline that. Don't ever be ashamed of honest accomplishment. If others don't understand, that's their problem. But if you deny what you are and how you became that, then it's yours, as well.

It wasn't a smooth sail from there. He had a stint as a life insurance salesman, a job at which he was admittedly horrible. But he met his wife at that job, and he realized during the hours when he was not selling insurance that what he wanted to be was a writer.

He begged an interview with an editor for the Westchester-Rockland newspapers in suburban New York. The editor told him he wasn't a college graduate and therefore did not qualify. Walter asked him to explain by what criteria the editor decided which writers to promote and which to let go. At the end of the explanation, Walter pointed out, "Not once did you mention a college education."

The editor hired him at a salary less than half of what Walter had been making at the insurance job. He didn't care. It was what he loved. "In every building on every street there is a story," he said. "And I wanted to get those stories and write them."

He went to school at Westchester Community College during the days and worked nights, and in two years he was both a valedictorian and an editor. In two more years, he was the valedictorian at Mercy College, and soon after that he was managing editor of the chain and was teaching journalism.

Never looking back, never accepting that there was anything he couldn't do, Walter kept moving up until he landed at *Parade*, which he remade into his own version of his beloved *Life* magazine.

Over the years, he tried to find Ilza Williams and her son, Barry, to tie together the strings connecting his past to his present. Finally, in 1993 he asked *Parade*'s investigative reporter, Bernard Gavzer, to try to find them.

Within two weeks Gavzer had found Mrs. Williams just a couple of miles away from Walter's home. And he gave Walter a phone number in San Francisco for Barry, who, it turned out, had not only graduated at the top of his class from both Harvard Business School and Harvard Law School, but had also established basketball scoring records at Harvard that stood for decades.

Reunited with his childhood mentor, Walter let her know that he had turned out all right after all, and that her belief in him had sustained him. He asked her to accompany him to a testimonial honoring him that was being given by the Massachusetts Society for the Prevention of Cruelty to Children. She was unable to attend, but she sent a videotape for him to play.

On the tape she spoke of those days when her backyard was the neighborhood safe harbor. She said of Walter, "He cursed the loudest, fought the most, and stayed the longest."

It would be a good epitaph for Walter Anderson were it not that he has another in mind.

"What I want on my tombstone," he says, "is, 'First, he was a Marine.' "

PART FIVE

Moments of Truth Lie in Realizing What Really Matters

Several years ago, I almost died. I had a kidney stone, and when it passed through my kidney, it blocked the ureter leading to my bladder. Only then did I and my doctors learn that I had only one functioning kidney—the one that was now blocked.

A priest gave me the last rites, and I truly thought I wouldn't make it out of the hospital. My kids came to see me and told me about the hundreds of phone calls that had been coming in from all over the country, asking about me. The room was full of flowers. I remember sitting there, thinking that was probably the most satisfying experience of all, having people care about me. I thought about Arthur Miller's play Death of a Salesman, *in which Willy Loman dies and no one comes to the funeral, and how I had so many people who cared about me.*

When you can see death, you realize that the important

things do not cost anything, that money truly isn't important. All my life, I have tried to help others, to give back to society for all the things society has given me. I have helped hundreds of people find jobs and have mentored scores of young people. I have a black belt in karate and I have also taught the martial arts to dozens of young people who were small and insecure and felt picked on. I was a small kid myself, and I understand how powerless you can feel. Karate gave me confidence, so I have helped instill that confidence in others.

That's what the stories in this section are about—discovering what really matters in life, the projects and goals that make you feel good about yourself because they reach out to others.

My friend Tom Volz spent his life chasing material goods and success, but it was only when he was faced with the loss of his life through cancer that he realized that happiness was inside him and he only had to look there to find it.

Paul Burns experienced his Moment of Truth as a teenager when he found that happiness was derived from his own soul and not from the opinions of his peers.

Singer Celine Dion faced a Moment of Truth when a beloved niece died in her arms, and Celine realized that her money and fame were meaningless unless she used them to help others.

Finally, there is Joni Davis, who saw her Moment of Truth in the eyes of an abused little girl. In that Moment, Joni realized that her own dream of a job that paid well was not nearly as important as giving needy and neglected children an opportunity to thrive.

In discovering what really matters, these four people are making a difference in our world.

Thomas Volz

Tom Volz began life as a child of privilege. When his family lost everything, he seemed to adjust. He emerged as an adult with a driving ambition to pursue the things that he thought would make him happy, whether in the form of money, partying, or affairs. He had a lot of fun and many adventures, but even more heartache. He never found contentment until he was told he had terminal cancer. When faced with death, he discovered life. He doesn't know how much time he has left, but he's making the most of it and enjoying it more than he ever thought possible.

He was born, he admits, with a silver spoon in his mouth, the happy resident of a big house on a hill with five cars in the driveway in the little town of Winner, South Dakota.

Tom Volz's father, Harold, was a businessman and a

politician. His mother was the perfect wife, keeping a spotless house, organizing dinner parties for the important people with whom her husband associated. There was even talk of Harold Volz making a run for governor.

Harold first ran for the state house in 1948, when Tom, the younger of the two Volz boys, was five. Harold lost, but didn't quit. When he started to think about running again in the early 1950s, his opponents looked for a way to derail his candidacy.

They found it in a construction company that Harold had started. Harold, they learned, was helping with the down payments for some of the homes, which were financed by the federal government. That was a conflict of interest and a federal crime. He was charged, tried, convicted, and sent to federal prison for two years.

Just like that, young Tom's silver spoon turned to plastic. Not only did the case eat up the family fortune, but it drove them out of the state, to Santa Monica, California, where Jeannette Volz had family. It was 1956 and Tom, just five feet tall and ninety pounds soaking wet, was turning thirteen years old.

The move was wrenching for everyone. Jeannette didn't even have a driver's license and now she found herself needing to support her family. She was lucky to get together with a bandleader named Lawrence Welk, a fellow South Dakotan whom she had known in happier days. As Welk became the star of a popular television show, Jeannette became his personal secretary.

But money was still tight. To pay tuition at the Catholic high school they attended, the boys took jobs as janitors. It wasn't a job that impressed the pampered sons and daughters of the movie stars they went to school with.

"They sent the school bully after me," Tom says. "I whipped him."

You can still hear a defiant teenage swagger in his voice. Life had dumped on him and it hurt. Being poor and skinny in a school full of the pampered and privileged increased the hurt. Tom became more aggressive, more eager to prove his worth. Those who react that way often become successful. But the success doesn't necessarily cure the deep wounds.

At the time, it was enough to survive from day to day and to build a new life. The education Tom received in his new circumstances extended far beyond the classroom. "That's where I learned to champion the underdog," he says. "It's where I learned the difference between the haves and the have-nots."

It is something that only one who has been there can honestly say. "Sure, there was a lot of anger," Tom says. "But there was no sense sitting on the pity-pot. My mother always told us, 'Don't think you're too good to work. And if you're going to push a broom, be the best broom pusher you can be.' So none of us were afraid of working.

"What I learned then was that the world can be a roller coaster," Tom says. "I developed real survival instincts."

Tom worked harder than he ever had. He went out for sports, and, blessed with outstanding speed, he was a champion sprinter and the captain of the football team by the time he was a senior. He was also student body president. He had an outgoing personality and a wealth of charm, and another way he overcompensated was by dating the daughters of some of the best-known people in show business. Maybe he wasn't rich anymore, but he was going to show he could compete.

Meanwhile, Tom's father had come home from prison. He was no longer the hale and hearty man he had been. He got a job with an insurance company and fell into a depression. Tom had another reason to prove he wasn't a loser.

He won a track scholarship to San Jose State, where he studied broadcasting. But to support himself, he took a job with United Airlines as a ticket agent and decided he liked the airline business. After college, he went into United's management training program.

Tom figured he had put the bad days behind him. He was eager, personable, and ambitious, and he skittered up the corporate ladder until he was stationed in Chicago as the airlines' national convention manager. It was a fun job for a young man with a zest for life, the kind of job that involved a lot of entertaining.

One night, he took the entertaining too far and embarrassed his employers. "I thought I was being drunk and charming, but I was really drunk and stupid," he says.

Tom was hauled onto the corporate carpet for his excess and was handed a demotion. United also transferred him from its Chicago corporate headquarters to New York City, where in quick succession he met a model, fell in love, got married, and had his first child, Elizabeth.

"Life was going along well," he says. They were living in the city, where he was marketing manager for the Northeast, and he had undertaken to get back into good physical shape after a decade of too much drink and too many good times. But after twelve years with United Airlines, he wasn't making enough money to enjoy the lifestyle he and his wife felt they had earned.

He was still out to prove his worth to the world, and that was measured in getting back all the things he had been denied by his father's mistake. He was successful, but he wasn't happy.

He thought a new job in the hotel business with a better salary in his wife's home state of Tennessee would fix everything. But jobs and money can't fix what's broken inside you. Tom got a hint of that in his new position. "I took it for the money," he says, "and it didn't work out."

So in 1978 he changed jobs again. He had spent twelve good and stable years with United, but he was now embarking on a journey that would take him from one job to another to another—all in the airline industry.

At first he thought he was back in heaven. He was working for Southwest Airlines in Dallas. His wife loved the Texas social life, and he was winning marketing awards and getting raises. He felt so good he even gave up drinking and got himself in shape.

But a great life was never good enough for Tom. He never realized it—how many of us do?—but he was still trying to own the world. Instead of being grateful for what he had, he wanted more.

"My wife and I thought we were living more modestly than we deserved," he says. "I started looking for job offers. One came along that was the classic offer I couldn't refuse.

"It turned into a catastrophe."

The job was vice president of marketing with Continental Airlines, then owned by one of the legendary ogres of the airline business, Frank Lorenzo. Everyone told Tom that he would be lucky to last a year with Lorenzo, who went through executives like M&M's. But the job was for double his salary at Southwest, and it included stock options.

"I've never owned a boat," Tom says, "but people tell me that there are two great days when you do—the day you buy it and the day you sell it. It was like that at Continental. I lasted about a year, which was twice as long as most people lasted there. It was a very, very long time."

Lorenzo fired him, as he fired most of his executives. "I'd never been fired before," Tom says, "but being fired by Frank Lorenzo was sort of a badge of honor. It was not a blot on my résumé."

Still, he was out of work, and this time it wasn't of his choosing. For a long time Tom had been climbing, but now he started to fall.

It was 1985 and his third child, Cathy, had just been born. At a time when he should have been enjoying the security of seniority and a good job, he was job hunting. He moved to Denver for a job with People Express. When that outfit went belly-up, he moved to Las Vegas to work for a nine-plane outfit called Sun World, but this time as upper management with a chance to own a part of the airline.

This looked like the opportunity Tom had always wanted. He had a big house with three cars and a nanny to look after the kids. He threw his own money into the operation and lost it all. By 1988 he was on the street with no job, no severance, no money, and a marriage that was falling apart.

He and his wife separated. She went back to Dallas and he stayed in Las Vegas, trying to find happiness in shallow affairs with women, scraping along on whatever job he could find. A year earlier he had been one of the hottest up-and-coming executives in town. Now he was working as a publicist in a six-by-eight-foot office on the mezzanine of the bowling alley in Sam's Town, a blue-collar casino.

"It was humbling," Tom says, "but I wasn't embarrassed."

He also hadn't learned anything. As soon as he could find a job with an airline, he took it. But whenever he hired on with a new company, it went bankrupt. Finally, after another failed venture in Australia, he learned his lesson.

"I got a job with the Dallas Convention and Visitors Bureau," he says. "I knew they weren't going to go out of business." It wasn't big money, but it was good work. He thought he was happy.

He was kidding himself. He took the job because he was worn-out, not because he'd had an awakening. Underneath, he still wanted to be a big shot, still wanted to show everyone that Tom Volz wasn't a loser. Despite bankruptcy and the dissolution of his marriage, he still hadn't gotten a grasp on what was really important. To Tom, it was still material success.

So when, in 1993, an old friend from the airline business called and said, "Let's start an airline somewhere," Tom said, "Sure."

This time, it was South Carolina and a start-up called Air South. For a change, everything seemed to be working.

After the first year, they were nearly at the break-even point and were talking about going public.

Tom felt great. He started running again and decided that he was going to compete in master's track for athletes over fifty. But before he started heavy training, he underwent a complete physical. He checked out perfectly except for an elevated score in the blood test for Prostate Specific Antigen—PSA.

The doctor said it was probably nothing, but recommended a biopsy. The results came back positive. Tom's prostate was riddled with cancer.

"This was my Moment of Truth," Tom says. "After everything I'd been through, when I got to the word 'cancer'—knowing that prostate cancer isn't curable if it metastasizes—I was staring straight down the gun barrel.

"I didn't think I was immortal," he says, "but I thought if I kept getting knocked down and kept getting back up, something good should happen. This was absolutely earth-shattering. I couldn't understand it at all. I was bewildered. It was illogical."

It didn't make sense because he had spent his life fighting the good fight. His father's being sent to prison was his test, and he had passed it. But there was no arguing with medical fact. He had spent his life chasing a chimera of material success, and just when it seemed within his grasp, he found it was meaningless in the face of possible death.

He underwent surgery to remove his prostate in February 1996. While he was recuperating, Tom had a lot of time to think about where he had been and what lay ahead. He decided that he wanted to do something that didn't derive its meaning from money or a job. The South Carolina Seniors Track Championships were in May. He set his sights on getting into good enough shape to simply run in the 100- and 200-meter dashes.

"I didn't care where I finished," he says. "I showed up that day, and I won 'em both—the one hundred meters and the two hundred meters. And I finished second in the discus and third in the long jump, and qualified for the Senior Olympics.

"That was one of the neatest days of my life."

For the first time in years, he had found pure enjoyment in simple personal accomplishment. It had taken cancer to show him that fulfillment has nothing to do with your bank account or the number of bathrooms in your house.

While he was recuperating, his new airline went bankrupt, but he didn't care as he always had before. He had awakened to the true meaning of life. He took a job as CEO and president of the Columbia, South Carolina, Visitors and Convention Bureau and started taking life one day at a time. His kids were grown, and if he felt like going to visit one of them, he didn't put it off. He did it. If he thought of a friend, he called instead of waiting. The cancer had taught him a lesson that thirty years of living couldn't—that life is finite, and we can be certain only of today.

In 1997 his cancer returned. The doctors gave him five months to life. More than two and a half years later, he was still alive and kicking, still running track, still living life better than he ever had before. He met a woman who shared his passion for life and formed a deeper and more mature relationship with her than any he had had before.

Dying now holds no terror for him. He came to terms with it long ago. "It's not the fear of death that bothers me," he says. "It's not the pain that comes at the end. It's failing to live through the process. And I really mean to live in a celebratory fashion."

He invents reasons to celebrate and creative ways to do it. When he turned 55 in 1998, he woke up at 5:55 A.M., ran 5.5 miles, swam 550 meters, biked 5.5 miles, walked 5.5 kilometers with 5-pound weights in his hands, and, in the evening, as near to 5:55 P.M. as he could manage it, he did a free fall out of an airplane with an instructor for 55 seconds.

"It was an absolutely phenomenal experience," he says, and he intends to repeat it.

He's a good friend, and neither he nor I know if he'll be alive to read this book. But whether he is or isn't, he knows he'll enjoy what time he has.

"There's a phenomenal upside to this," he says of the process of dying. "I don't have to prove anything to anybody. I have a son in college and a daughter in the ninth grade. I have plenty of insurance, so I don't have to worry about taking care of them financially.

"I work from eight to five, not from eight to eleven. If I have unfinished business with people, I close that. If I have somewhere to go, I go there."

He wants to live today, and he will. He'll worry about tomorrow when and if it gets here.

PAUL BURNS

———

As a kid, Paul Burns was a searcher, a dreamer, a young man who wanted to be noticed. At first, he thought the way to get attention was to be a juvenile delinquent. The love of his father saved him from that, and the love of God pointed him in a new direction. It led him from a comfortable suburban life in New Jersey into a career living among and serving the homeless. The work tries his body and soul every day, but it also gives him rewards he wouldn't trade for all the adulation in the world.

There was nothing in Paul Burns's childhood to predict that he would devote his life to helping the homeless. He had an ordinary childhood, a big, loving family, and no memories of abandonment that would make him turn to others who felt alone.

Paul was born in 1960, the sixth of nine children—four boys and five girls—in an Irish Catholic family. Eight of the children were born to Joseph and Patricia Burns in a comfortable little New Jersey town packed cheek by jowl with two-story wood-frame houses. As if eight were not enough, the Burns also adopted a Puerto Rican girl who had lost her family in a fire. Her addition to the family helped instill in Paul an ethic of helping those less fortunate than himself.

Paul's father and mother both worked. Joseph commuted by bus to Manhattan, where he was an insurance executive. Patricia taught in the local school system. The stereotype of insurance executives is one of pin-striped conservatism, but Joseph had a social conscience that he passed on to his family.

Paul remembers going with his father to Harlem to help set up block parties and paint houses. Joseph also took him to rallies for a variety of social causes. "We were all encouraged to pursue what was closest to our hearts," Paul says. "My father was bohemian. He brought us to antiwar protests. He made us aware of social activism."

All the children attended parochial schools, and their Catholic faith was a big part of their lives. But at the age of ten, Paul changed. With his next-oldest brother, who was eleven, Paul began turning into what he calls a juvenile delinquent. Looking back, he sees himself as a kid looking for attention.

It sometimes happens that way in big families. Kids in the middle, though provided for and surrounded by people who care, can still feel lost. If they're not the type to assert themselves and outstrip the others in the battle for attention, they can turn away.

Paul did that. He became a problem kid in school. The parochial school expelled him, and in the public schools he fell in with a gang of kids who were practicing to be dropouts. This was 1970, the age of free love, flower power, and marijuana, and Paul's peer group looked up to the boys a couple of years older than they who were already drinking beer and toking up.

By the time he was fourteen, Paul was known by the local police as a troublemaker and he had a rap sheet in juvenile court.

If his behavior was a cry for attention, he got it. Paul says his father "let me know it wasn't going to be that way for me. He spent a lot of time with me and barred me from seeing those kids."

Love helped him find his way. The pain he had caused his family made Paul look inside himself and consider the direction in which he was headed. He decided he didn't want to run with the drugs-and-beer crowd. He wanted something more.

"My dad helped me realize I was jeopardizing my life," he says. "He let me know he wasn't going to put up with me continuing to go the way I was going."

Divorced from his old gang, Paul looked for a new peer group. He found it in a local coffeehouse run by evangelical Christians. The establishment sponsored a Bible study group that met regularly and Paul was invited to join. He accepted.

The group showed him another way. Something clicked deep in his soul, and Paul knew that he had found a home.

It was his first Moment of Truth. He was fourteen, an age that's often an important turning point for kids. His experience reminds all of us who have children that teenagers especially need us when they are most difficult to like.

"I dedicated my life to becoming a Christian," Paul says. "I thought that if Christianity was going to enable me to have a better life, it would give me a better chance to get through high school, to have the strength to study. It brought me great peace and understanding through a personal commitment. I didn't have to be afraid of bullies or of being an outcast. I could trust God."

In many Catholic homes, Paul's turn toward evangelical Christianity would have been seen as a calamity almost as great as—if not greater than—his troubles with the law. The Catholicism that Paul's parents grew up with held that only Catholics could be saved, and it was a mortal sin to consort with other Christian denominations. Breaking the law could be forgiven. Heresy was a different matter.

But Paul was fortunate in that his parents, particularly his father, valued what was in a person's heart more than doctrine. Joseph didn't approve of his son's new religion, but what Paul was doing with his life was more important. "My father is an independent spirit," says Paul. "He would tell me what he thought of my faith, but hug me and tell me to keep up the good job."

He became a model student, a stand-out two-miler on the track team and an exceptional cross-country runner, good enough to be among the top ten in New Jersey. But something else besides the normal high school life of study, sports, and parties called to him. He didn't know why or how the call came to him. It just did.

When he was sixteen, he followed his heart. He went to the bus station in the neighboring town of Hackensack and got on a bus bound for the 178th Street Port Authority bus terminal. From there, he took subways down to the Lower East Side, to the Bowery. Just a skinny kid from Jersey, shining and innocent, he carried with him the New Testament and a bag of fruit.

"It was a strong, indescribable magnet that pulled me there," he says. "I walked down there at first to bring some good news and fellowship to people who had absolutely nothing else in their lives, no hope. I wanted to share my faith and try to help people any way I could."

Asked to explain why, Paul is almost at a loss. He only knows that it had something to do with the path he had been headed on before he found meaning in his life. "I saw that God had spared me from that future," he says. "There but for the grace of God . . ."

That launched him on his life's work. He went to a Bible college, met a street missionary from New York, and accepted an invitation to join a ministry in the City. He worked first in the projects of Staten Island, then in a Times Square mission, ladling soup, saving souls, giving comfort. He had no money, but he was happy.

He learned about life in the streets and how to survive there armed with nothing but the Good Book. He also learned that a church isn't a building but an attitude, a state of mind.

"This was a profound insight, and I realized that you can have a church in the middle of a wealthy New Jersey suburb or in the middle of Bedford-Stuyvesant. A church is a building that people go into to worship. But you can also have a ministry on the street. That connection of spirit out on the street is very gratifying."

It is also very draining, with the pain and the hopelessness and the loneliness constantly eating away at you. After several years at the mission, Paul's spirit started to show the strain.

He had met and befriended a man in his sixties who lived in a ground-floor apartment in a building that had been purchased by developers. His name was Jim Webb and he had grown up in Georgia and lived for a time in Pennsylvania. He was six foot two and two hundred pounds, and was still strong and vigorous. By the time he washed up in New York, he had no one. No friends, no family.

Although Jim paid his rent and was living in the tiny apartment legally, the new owners planned to renovate the building and turn it into condominiums for the Yuppies who were then reclaiming many such neighborhoods.

Jim had been told by unfriendly-looking men to move out, but the little apartment and a cat he kept as a pet were all he had, and he wasn't going to give them up. He couldn't find another rent-controlled apartment as cheap as that one, and, anyway, it was the only home he knew. For years, the cat was the only friend he had had.

That changed when Paul found him in the streets and offered his help. "He wanted to make a confession," Paul says. "It was hard for him to talk to a minister or social worker. But people sense they can tell me anything they want. He wanted to talk about the bad checks he wrote that put him in jail, about all the things he had done. He wasn't a bad man, and he was happy just to get it out."

One day Paul got word that Jim had been run over in the street—a hit-and-run accident that Paul had no doubt was meant to get him out of the building, permanently. A weaker man might have died. But, despite multiple fractures and internal injuries, Jim survived, and when he was discharged from the hospital, he stubbornly moved back into his home.

There are times to minister to the spirit and times to minister to the body. This was one of the latter times, and Paul knew he had to get Jim out of that building. But the old man wouldn't budge. He had decided that if they wanted him out, they would have to kill him.

The thugs were up to the challenge. Some time after Jim recovered from the hit-and-run, he landed in the hospital again, his body punctured by multiple stab wounds. Again, he should have died. Again he didn't.

Paul visited Jim in the hospital, held his hand, ached inside when Jim grabbed hold of his hand, squeezed it hard, and smiled at him through the haze of drugs.

Again Jim recovered, and Paul took him home. Together, they helped Jim's cat deliver a litter of kittens. They shared the joy of new life and cuddled the kittens, naming them together. "You've got to get out of here," Paul told Jim.

"He refused to go," Paul told me.

Finally, Jim was killed in a fire set by arsonists.

Jim's death hit Paul so hard that he left New York and

moved back to New Jersey. "That was the first bonding I had with the dark side. The dark, dull pain that you never lose," he says.

Paul had only one consolation, that at least Jim had found God and inner peace before he died. "That's why I always return to the streets," Paul says. "You can't keep going at it with the same energy all the time. Those things definitely do a number on you. In the end, you walk a walk and talk a talk and that's all there is. There's a peace that comes with that."

He never really left the street ministry; he just moved to a different area. Looking around affluent Bergen County, New Jersey, where he grew up and now lived, he saw that even in that place there were homeless. Unlike the homeless in New York, they had virtually no one who cared about them.

Paul calls it his second Moment of Truth. With renewed energy, he walked the streets of Hackensack, New Jersey, living in a spare apartment without a television, with virtually no comforts. "I felt it was important to live like they did," he says.

He came to identify strongly with John the Baptist, the wild evangelist who ate locusts in the desert, and, indeed, Paul does have a lot of the wild man in him. He is passionate about his work and his people. But for several years no one would listen to him. People in the suburbs were much less receptive to his message. Their attitude was that if you took care of homeless people, you'd be stuck with them.

Then, in 1994, a local homeless man was bludgeoned to death in a public park by a gang of kids out to steal his Social Security check. The brutality of the crime galvanized the county, and Paul used the new awareness to secure funding to build a homeless shelter. For his efforts, he won a humanitarian award that brought with it a check for $50,000.

Paul considered the check a down payment on his next project—group homes for those homeless people who are most capable of moving back into mainstream society. Paul intends to call the home Salt of the Earth.

"In the end, the Lord is the salt of the earth," he says. "He's the blessing and seasoning of the earth. It is of the earth, not what's built on the earth."

"Twenty years is a long time to be doing this," he says. At times, he has been tempted to stop. But he met a woman at church, Carmen Colon, and fell in love with her. They plan to marry. "She has eight beautiful kids," he says. "She has lived the hardest life you can imagine."

Carmen gave him the balance he needed in his life. "I was losing my ability to continue my work until I met her," he says. "But she refused to let me be consumed by Salt of the Earth. She permitted me to be Paul Burns again."

She made him whole and continues to give him the strength to continue his crusade. Every day of my life, I thank God for people like Paul Burns.

CELINE DION

―――――――――

She is, as they say, a woman who needs no introduction. The story of how Celine Dion put her own singing career on hold to help her husband battle cancer is familiar to most people. What I didn't know is how uncommonly approachable and caring for others Celine truly is. It isn't an act. She is that rarest of people—a superstar who puts others before herself. Nor did I suspect that her Moment of Truth came well before her husband's illness, when she rushed home from a concert to help her favorite niece make the passage from this life to the next. It was a great loss for Celine, but she came to know through her niece's far too brief existence how precious life is. Through her tireless work for charity, Celine has made her own loss a gain for uncounted others.

Life is a gift. So, too, is death.

It is not easy for any of us to understand that, let alone a twenty-five-year-old woman who has led a life of joy and vibrancy, untouched by most of the stresses of the real world. But Celine Dion is an extraordinary woman who knows such truths instinctively. The knowledge is the source of the emotion that she puts into the songs she sings. With them, she can hold 100,000 people spellbound.

Think about that the next time you hear Celine wrap her voice around a song and touch you deep inside. Know that she can do that because she once held in her arms a dying child whom she loved. In that Moment of Truth, she understood that love is more important than wealth and talent.

In 1993 Celine was twenty-five and just beginning to become an international superstar. In the same year her beloved niece Karine, who had lived sixteen difficult but full years, died of cystic fibrosis.

Karine had always been there to remind Celine that not everyone's life is charmed and that the same fates that gave Celine a beautiful voice gave others suffering and indignity.

Celine was nine when her sister, Liette, gave birth to Karine. Just two months later, the doctors told Karine's parents that their beautiful baby girl had cystic fibrosis, a disease that clogs the lungs and other organs with mucus. They were told she would not live a long and healthy life.

That was in 1977, and the girl who would grow up to open the Olympic Games in Atlanta, sing the themes to *Beauty and the Beast*, *Sleepless in Seattle*, and *Titanic*, win Oscars and Grammys, circle the globe singing for clamoring audiences, and become an international celebrity was already marked for stardom. She had sung in public for the first time at the age of five at her brother's wedding, and she was consumed by a passion for music and performing on stage.

Her eight sisters and five brothers encouraged her, as did her mother, who was an exceptional musician in her own right. They would hand her a pen or a comb and stand her on the table, and little Celine would hold the object like a microphone and sing her heart out. When her father bought a bar, she stood on tables and sang there, to the delight of the patrons. By the time she was twelve, anyone who heard her knew that she was destined for greatness.

By any account except her own, she grew up poor in the small town of Charlemagne just east of Montreal, Canada. As the last of fourteen children, and the youngest by six years, she never lacked for the things that matter most to a child—love, attention, approval, and encouragement. To her, her childhood was perfect. Although her clothes were hand-me-downs, the love she received was always new and original.

"At home, there was love, music, a food smell, affection," she once told an interviewer. "People were everywhere, there was singing, my mother was cooking her own bread and I was so happy—I was the baby of the family, very spoiled, just like I am now. It was a great childhood. I rarely went out, but you don't need to go out when people are fighting about who's going to bathe you. Today, I feel like I'm singing for my family."

Along with the love, Celine also had the one thing that made her life whole—music. It seemed the entire family was born with music vibrating in their bones. It was all around her and inside her, perfect music in her heart, in her soul, in the souls of her parents and siblings, in the very timbers of the house that her parents had built themselves, board by board, wire by wire, pipe by pipe. And music ran deeper in Celine than in any of them.

I met Celine in 1999 in her home in Jupiter, Florida, a confident woman of thirty-one, sophisticated, beautiful, yet still as natural as the reflection of a cloud-dotted sky in a placid pond. Even then, after absorbing years of barbs written by cynical critics, after seeing her family quarrel over her success, after enduring the disapproval of people who saw something wrong with her marrying René Angelil, her manager and a twice-divorced man twenty-six years her senior, she found no flaws in the canvas of her life, felt no bitterness toward anyone, had no regrets.

And she didn't think she could teach others about life.

After all, as she points out, "I haven't really had the chance to learn about me."

I know better now. She had long since learned everything important.

It was summer when we met, and she had just begun her sabbatical from work to be with her husband, René, as he recovered from surgery and treatment to remove a malignancy from his neck. It was exceedingly difficult for her to watch this man whom she loved deeply become sick, yet not be able to do more to make him well.

"I would just love to take this thing, this disease, and just shake it up and do more with it, but I can't. So what I can do is try to go through this with him. Feel every moment with him. Every moment of pain and joy and suffering. Everything. I want to be able to do it with him."

Talking about René's disease led her to discuss her niece Karine.

"She died in my arms," Celine recalls.

She viewed the loss as the final installment of a gift that Karine had been giving her for all of the sick child's sixteen years on earth. It was the lesson that not everyone is born with equal talent or opportunity. It was the awareness that her talent is a gift that must be used to help others.

In her authorized biography, *Celine,* written by Georges-Herbert Germain, Celine talked about singing "The Power of the Dream" at the opening ceremonies for the 1996 Atlanta Olympic Games. The song was meant as a tribute to the athletes gathered there to compete, but Celine told Germain that the song troubled her.

"The truth is that for lots of people, it's not like that at all. Some people don't have the luck, the skill, the talent. Some kids are born healthy, some are born sick or crippled. I wondered what Karine would have thought of this song. What would the kids who live in poverty . . . think about it?"

It is wonderful to have dreams, she realized. But she also knew that she was lucky because she had everything she needed to fulfill hers.

She had some of the greatest songwriters working for her, the backing of major corporations, and the vast reservoir of approval that her family had filled for her as a child. Celine admitted that she had her own dreams—"To sing on the world's greatest stages."

To some artists, the glory is all-important. But Celine learned through Karine that glory is reserved for the few and that the really important things are the small and ordinary comforts.

Celine flew to Montreal from London in early May 1993 to be by Karine's side when the girl went into her final decline. She helped her sister dress Karine in new pajamas, held her in her arms, and sang to her, an a cappella concert for one in a hospital room.

As Celine sang, Karine told her what she loved about life. She talked about special dinners, songs, clothes. "It was like an inventory, a kind of testament, a list of memories, as if she wanted to take the few beautiful things she'd known in life with her," Celine told me.

That's how Karine died—in Celine's arms and with Celine's voice ringing softly in her ear. "One tear came down Karine's cheek, and then she went," Celine says. "There are so many dangers in life, so much illness, so many accidents. Some of us are lucky, some aren't. That's one of the great mysteries of life.

"My life is a fairy tale, and I know it. But I know I live in a frightening world where thousands of children die of hunger every day. I don't want to forget. We can't forget."

Celine had always done what she could for Karine. When she was home, she would take her niece, oxygen bottles in tow, to the mall to shop. But as Karine grew weaker, she eventually was confined to bed, fighting for every breath she took. Seeing her like that was enormously difficult for Celine.

And then finally, there was no next breath.

Celine says, "Sometimes we might take things for granted, like the air and the sunshine and the rain and health, and you see those people suffering and you say, 'Oh, my God.' And when she died in my arms . . ." Here she paused. "It's the greatest gift that somebody gave me in a way, because she put me in contact with heaven."

That's when Celine had her Moment of Truth, when she understood the truth about life and death. "That was an incredible moment. And she definitely gave me a lot of strength. And it was a wonderful moment.

"I mean it's very painful," Celine says, explaining that in death Karine was finally free. "I said to myself, for the first time she's going to breathe, she's going to be okay."

I found as we talked that we shared not only an experience but also a deep faith that things happen for a reason, that there is a Providence that guides us, and that death is a tragedy only if we allow it to be. I shared with her the story of my own daughter's death. And we both understood that she, a young and beautiful superstar, and I, an old advertising and marketing executive, were more alike than either one of us would have thought.

JONI DAVIS

There is no greater love than that of a mother for her child, and few things more terrible than a mother who lacks that love. Joni Davis was an adopted child who grew up with an unusual awareness of the importance of that maternal bond. She got married young, divorced, and always dreamed of the time when her children would be grown and she could move from the small town in which she lived to a big city. But a Moment of Truth showed her that true happiness isn't a place in the world, but a place in the heart.

Joni Davis was eager to move away from Beaumont, Texas, the town where she grew up, was married, raised her children, got divorced. She was still young—in her early forties—and she had a knack for public relations and fund-raising. Austin, the state capital, was where she wanted to go.

But she kept seeing a pair of eyes so big and blue they looked as if they had been dipped out of the ocean. The eyes belonged to a face that was as pretty as Joni had ever seen on a ten-year-old girl, but they weren't happy eyes. They were open wide and darting this way and that around the foyer of the big house to which her mother had brought her.

The girl's name was Heather*, and the contrast between mother and daughter was enormous. Heather was frightened, the mother impatient. Heather, whose shoulder-length blond hair needed brushing, wore a dirty T-shirt and shorts too small for her, along with a pair of old sandals; the mother, whose big blond hairdo had come from an expensive salon, wore spiffy Wrangler jeans that looked as if they had been painted on, a blouse that hugged her curves, and a new pair of Roper boots.

Joni wasn't supposed to be greeting mother and daughter in the foyer of Girls' Haven, a home in Beaumont for girls who had no other place to go. Her job was in public relations and fund-raising. In fact, when she had taken the job a year earlier, part of the deal was that she avoid close contact with the girls. "They knew I'd get too personally involved," she says in her soft Texas drawl. "I wouldn't have that professional detachment you need to have."

But when you're dealing with kids, professional detachment isn't always possible. Every haven for battered and neglected children needs somebody who cares passionately about kids. In the blue eyes of that little girl Joni found her

* Name has been changed to protect the child's identity.

Moment of Truth and what would become the job for which she had always searched and never knew how to find.

The mother who dropped Heather off was in her late twenties and simply didn't want to be bothered with the girl. She seemed to lack even the tiniest shred of maternal love. Unwilling to pay for child care, and also unwilling to give up her partying social life, she often locked Heather in the bathroom of their house and left her there, sometimes all night. Finally, she brought Heather to Girls' Haven, which Dr. Mark Wilson and his wife, La Nell, along with a group of other prominent citizens of Beaumont, had founded in 1994. They bought a big old one-story residence that could sleep twelve girls and two houseparents. It was a fine house, with shiny hardwood floors, ten-foot ceilings, a big foyer, a huge living room, and a set of double front doors with etched-glass panels.

Joni had come to work there by accident. She and La Nell had been friends since high school. They stayed in touch because Joni had a knack with computers and press releases and graphics, and La Nell, heavily involved in charity work, often called on Joni when she needed help.

Joni didn't mind that there wasn't much pay in it. Money had never driven her. Back when she was married, and someone asked what she did for a living, her husband would joke, "If it pays money, Joni runs away."

When she was first married, she opened a country music club with her husband and his family. It was a lot of fun and even more headaches for four years, at which point they had had enough and sold it.

After that, Joni's husband went into the private security

business and Joni became a stay-at-home housewife, raising their two children, Josh and Nikki. But she was never far from whatever local charity needed help. Helping other people to find the fun that she found in life was deeply ingrained in her. For ten years, she volunteered at a rape crisis center and traveled around Beaumont and the surrounding country speaking to groups, raising funds and awareness. At every school her children attended, she joined the PTA and she served for a time as the president of all PTAs in the city.

She and her husband divorced after eighteen years of marriage, when the kids were almost old enough to be on their own. For the first time Joni found she had to earn her own living. She got a job as an aide in the local high school. Because the work involved kids, English, and computers, she loved it. "I'm a magnet for kids," she confesses. "I just love 'em. I always have. Even as a girl, I was always collecting the kids that nobody else wanted to hang out with.

"Maybe it's because I was adopted myself," she muses.

She tried several different jobs, never earning much more than enough to cover rent and groceries. But money was never more important to her than job satisfaction. She even tried working for herself, organizing events and doing public relations. She was good at it, but she hated working alone at home. "I have to have people around me," she says.

She was lucky in a way. Only one of her two children was still at home, and her husband made regular child support payments so she didn't have to take the biggest paycheck she could find and stick to a job she couldn't stand. It gave her time to do something everyone should have the luxury of doing—trying different jobs and finding one that matched her personality.

Joni finally found that job in 1996 when La Nell recommended that the directors of Girls' Haven hire her to handle public relations and fund-raising. The job didn't pay much, but it was steady work. Joni took it.

That's how she came to be at Girls' Haven when Heather arrived. The girl had been scheduled to show up sometime after 7 P.M., after the girls had eaten dinner and had settled down to do their homework.

"We don't like to bring them in earlier," Joni says, "because it is very wild around dinnertime. Girls have chores, homework, dinner—a very typical home atmosphere. We don't want a new girl to walk into that and feel overwhelmed. And I'm usually gone for the day by then."

But on this day Heather came early because her mother had a date and didn't want to be late. One of the girls came back to Joni's office and told her there was a new girl at the door. Joni asked where the director was. The girl said he was out. With the houseparents busy with dinner, there was no one else to take care of the new arrival, so Joni said she'd do it.

"When I rounded the corner to come into the foyer, she just caught my eye," Joni says. "It just floored me. She was standing in the corner of the foyer, clutching some clothes. Just two or three pairs of shorts and a T-shirt. She had beautiful blond hair to her shoulders, a creamy white complexion with the hugest blue eyes I've ever seen. And she was terrified. She was shaking. Her eyes were looking all around.

"I thought she was afraid of us," Joni goes on. "I thought she was afraid that this big machine of life was going on around her, and all these people were making decisions, and she was just a pawn, with no choice in any of it.

"I walked up to her, my heart beating wildly. I knelt down to her and she looked me straight in the eye," Joni says. "If there was ever a Moment of Truth in my life, that was it. There was so much pain and fear in her eyes. It ran through my head that this was a ten-year-old, and for a moment all her pain transferred to me and I could feel it. It felt like a freight train, she hurt so bad.

"In that moment I could feel how afraid she was, how nobody wanted her, how she was just a child, unable to help herself. And it hit me that there was a beating heart in there, and that I wasn't working for an organization. I was working for this child and the kids in the other room so that they could have a safe place.

"Where would they be if I didn't help?"

Joni almost tears up repeating the story. "Until that moment, this had just been a job," she says. "And then it became my life."

Joni didn't question this revelation. She had always dreamed about going to Austin, but now she knew that her happiness lay right there in Beaumont.

The little girl was still standing stock-still, eyes large with apprehension. "Wait right here, honey," Joni said.

"Yes, ma'am," said the girl.

Joni ran back to her office and collected a teddy bear her son had recently given her. She brought it back to the foyer, knelt down and asked Heather if she liked teddy bears.

"Yes, ma'am, I do."

When Joni gave her the bear, Heather wasn't sure she should take it. "It's yours, isn't it?" she said.

"My son gave it to me, but I'll give it to you and it will be our teddy bear," Joni said. At that, Heather clutched that bear with all her might.

"She looked back at her mom and looked at me and tugged on my shirt. She was trying to get me to come closer. I put my ear close to her mouth, and she whispered, 'Can I stay with you? I'm scared of her,' and she looked over her shoulder at her mother. My heart broke.

"The people children trust and love the most should be their mother and father, but she was willing to go with a perfect stranger because she didn't want to be with her mom."

Joni looked up at the mother, dressed for a night of clubbing, and resisted the urge to stand up and punch her. Instead, she looked at Heather and said, "Yes, baby, you can stay with us."

Usually, Joni says, parents bringing their daughters to Girls' Haven will ask to see the place, if only because they think that's what they should do. Some mothers are genuinely devastated when they leave their daughters. "They're women who have several kids and no money and they have to give one of them up. Imagine the agony those women go through, trying to decide which of their children they're going to give away."

Not Heather's mother. "Can I leave now?" she asked,

stomping her booted foot on the hard wood to emphasize her impatience. "I have a date."

Joni got the housemother, introduced her to Heather, and saw Heather off to be integrated into her new family. Then she turned to the mother and said, "If you need to go, just go."

She almost spat the words out, even though she knew how unprofessional that was. "I shouldn't have taken that attitude," Joni admits, "but I'd had this moment. All of a sudden I had a purpose, and this woman to me was a monster.

"I had a little girl of my own that I tucked into bed every night and loved more than life itself. There's no train I wouldn't lie down in front of to save her life, and I couldn't understand this mother's ability to disassociate herself from her child."

It was 1997 when Heather arrived. Joni's son was in the Navy and her daughter was two years away from graduating from high school. By 1999 both of Joni's children had moved out and begun lives of their own. But Joni was still in Beaumont, still earning not nearly enough money, still raising funds for Girls' Haven, still being a friend to girls who desperately needed one.

"I'm very protective of our girls," she says. "Sometimes they get labeled in the school system as being failures at home, as if there is something wrong with them, because they're not the same as all the rest of the girls. There are parents who don't want our girls to come to their homes and play with their daughters."

That's another project for Joni to work on, another reason to stay in Beaumont.

"I can't leave," says Joni. "I'm so connected to this work." She has made sacrifices—accepted less pay, turned down exciting job offers—but she knows what matters more. Giving girls like Heather a safe haven. Replacing the fear in their eyes with trust and hope.

The work provides many bittersweet moments. The day came when Heather was placed with a home in another part of the state. "That was the object," Joni says, "to get her into a home where she would be safe and nurtured." It wasn't easy saying good-bye. "Letting go of Heather was hard for me because I was so attached to her," Joni says.

But the satisfaction she feels knowing that Heather is thriving in her new home outweighs the sadness of missing her. And the knowledge that her work is absolutely vital provides Joni with all the happiness she could ever want.

The Next Moment of Truth: A Final Word from Tony

All of us have Moments of Truth, some small, some large, some fleeting, some lingering. They can be sudden and jarring or they can be waiting for us calmly at the end of a long struggle. What I learned while writing this book is that it doesn't matter if we recognize such moments when they happen. More important is how we react when a crisis or an opportunity comes our way. If we are alert to the people and events with which we come in contact, and remain true to ourselves, we will be ready for whatever life throws in our path. And when we look back, we may realize that we have lived a Moment of Truth.

I have learned that a crisis is also an opportunity. There are lessons to be learned in death as well as in life. I honestly believe that that which does not kill us makes us stronger.

Life is a wonderful, brief journey. Every day is a blessing. True satisfaction comes from giving of ourselves to help others.

The people whose stories I have told here testify to that truth every day of their lives.

I intend to dedicate a large share of the profits from this book to establishing a foundation dedicated to helping people through their Moments of Truth. In some cases, that aid will be monetary. In others, it will take the form of guidance and consulting services. My hope is that through this book the foundation can grow sufficiently to reach people not just in the United States but also in other lands.

I don't want anyone to feel alone in a time of crisis. In some small way, I hope the Moment of Truth Foundation will help make that desire a reality.

Author Bios

Tony Wainwright, vice chairman of advertising agency McKinney & Silver, has professional and personal relationships with people all over the world through his lifelong career in advertising, where he introduced such products as StoveTop Stuffing Mix and Oil of Olay. He serves as a member on many boards of directors, is well known for his constant travels, and continues to work tirelessly raising funds for various charities.

Mike Celizic, a sports writer and commentator, has won numerous awards for journalism, was nominated for a Pulitzer Prize, and has appeared on various television news programs. He is the author or coauthor of six previous books.